THE COUNCIL OF LIVING SAINTS

The Meditations Of A Christian Saint

Agyeman Bonsu

Copyright © 2023 by Agyeman Bonsu All rights reserved.

No part of this book may be reproduced, distributed, or transmitted in any form or by any means, including photocopying, recording, or other electronic or mechanical methods, without the prior written permission of the publisher, or author except as permitted by U.S. copyright law.

Disclaimer

This work is an expression of the author's (Council of Living Saints) interpretations, revelations, and opinions. It is not intended to provide official religious, legal, or any other form of professional advice. Readers should consult authoritative religious or legal sources when seeking guidance on specific matters. The author and publisher accept no responsibility for any consequences arising from using or misusing the content herein.

DEDICATION

To my beloved wife,

This book is dedicated to you as a testament to the strength of our union and the profound impact of your presence on my spiritual journey.

To our precious children,

As you grow and explore the world, may the timeless wisdom within these pages serve as a source of guidance and inspiration on your unique paths.

To all our friends, acquaintances, and relatives,

We dedicate this book to you with gratitude for your support, encouragement, and the shared moments that have shaped our faith and understanding.

And to all the souls we have yet to meet,

As we embark on the future, may the words within these pages be a bridge of connection and wisdom, offering guidance and inspiration to all those who cross our paths.

With boundless love and anticipation,

Agyeman Bonsu.

The Council Of Living Saints
The Meditations Of A Christian Saint

CONTENTS

Introduction 1
Chapter 1 10
A Christian Saint 10
Chapter 2 15
The Character of a Saint 15
Chapter 3 17
Embracing the Identity of a Living Saint Implications 17
Chapter 4 22
Council of Living Saints 22
Chapter 5 25
The Human Fallen State or Condition 25
Chapter 6 32
Overcoming individual weaknesses 32
Chapter 7 37
1-Meditation 37
2-Meditation 37
3-Meditation 37
4-Meditation 37
5-Meditation 38
6-Meditation 38
7-Meditation 38
8-Meditation 38
9-Meditation 39
10-Meditation 39
11-Meditation 39
12-Meditation 39
13-Meditation 39
14-Meditation 40
15-Meditation 40
16-Meditation 40
17-Meditation 40
18-Meditation 41
19-Meditation 41
20-Meditation 41
21-Meditation 42
22-Meditation 42
23-Meditation 42
24-Meditation 42
25-Meditation 43

26-Meditation 43
27-Meditation 43
28-Meditation 44
29-Meditation 44
30-Meditation 44
31-Meditation 44
32-Meditation 46
33-Meditation 46
34-Meditation 46
35-Meditation 47
36-Meditation 47
37-Meditation 47
38-Meditation 47
39-Meditation 47
40-Meditation 48
41-Meditation 48
42-Meditation 48
43-Meditation 48
44-Meditation 48
45-Meditation 49
46-Meditation 49
47-Meditation 49
48-Meditation 49
49-Meditation 49
50-Meditation 50
51-Meditation 50
52-Meditation 50
53-Meditation 50
54-Meditation 51
55-Meditation 51
56-Meditation 51
57-Meditation 52
58-Meditation 52
59-Meditation 52
60-Meditation 52
61-Meditation 53
62-Meditation 53
63-Meditation 53
64-Meditation 53
65-Meditation 54
66-Meditation 54
67-Meditation 54
68-Meditation 54
69-Meditation 55

The Council Of Living Saints
The Meditations Of A Christian Saint

70-Meditation 55
71-Meditation 55
72-Meditation 55
73-Meditation 55
74-Meditation 56
75-Meditation 56
76-Meditation 56
77-Meditation 56
78-Meditation 57
79-Meditation 57
80-Meditation 57
81-Meditation 57
82-Meditation 57
83-Meditation 58
84-Meditation 58
85-Meditation 58
86-Meditation 58
87-Meditation 59
88-Meditation 59
89-Meditation 59
90-Meditation 59
91-Meditation 59
92-Meditation 60
93-Meditation 60
94-Meditation 60
95-Meditation 61
96-Meditation 61
97-Meditation 61
98-Meditation 62
99-Meditation 62
100-Meditation 62
101-Meditation 62
102-Meditation 63
103-Meditation 63
104-Meditation 64
105-Meditation 64
106-Meditation 64
107-Meditation 64
108-Meditation 65
109-Meditation 65
110-Meditation 65

111-Meditation 65
112-Meditation 67
113-Meditation 67
114-Meditation 67
115-Meditation 68
116-Meditation 68
117-Meditation 68
118-Meditation 68
119-Meditation 68
120-Meditation 68
121-Meditation 69
122-Meditation 69
123-Meditation 69
124-Meditation 69
125-Meditation 70
126-Meditation 70
127-Meditation 70
128-Meditation 71
129-Meditation 72
130-Meditation 72
131-Meditation 72
132-Meditation 73
133-Meditation 73
134-Meditation 73
135-Meditation 73
136-Meditation 73
137-Meditation 74
138-Meditation 74
139-Meditation 74
140-Meditation 74
141-Meditation 75
142-Meditation 75
143-Meditation 75
144-Meditation 75
145-Meditation 75
146-Meditation 76
147-Meditation 76
148-Meditation 76
149-Meditation 76
150-Meditation 76
151-Meditation 77
152-Meditation 77
153-Meditation 77
154-Meditation 77

The Council Of Living Saints
The Meditations Of A Christian Saint

155-Meditation 77
156-Meditation 78
157-Meditation 78
158-Meditation 78
159-Meditation 78
160-Meditation 79
161-Meditation 79
162-Meditation 79
163-Meditation 79
164-Meditation 80
165-Meditation 80
166-Meditation 80
167-Meditation 80
168-Meditation 80
169-Meditation 81
170-Meditation 81
171-Meditation 81
172-Meditation 81
173-Meditation 82
174-Meditation 82
175-Meditation 82
176-Meditation 82
177-Meditation 82
178-Meditation 83
179-Meditation 83
180-Meditation 83
181-Meditation 83
182-Meditation 84
183-Meditation 84
184-Meditation 84
185-Meditation 84
186-Meditation 85
187-Meditation 85
188-Meditation 85
189-Meditation 85
190-Meditation 85
200-Meditation 86
201-Meditation 86
202-Meditation 86
203-Meditation 86
204-Meditation 87

205-Meditation	87
206-Meditation	87
207-Meditation	87
208-Meditation	87
209-Meditation	88
210-Meditation	88
211-Meditation	88
212-Meditation	88
213-Meditation	88
214-Meditation	89
215-Meditation	89
216-Meditation	90
217-Meditation	90
218-Meditation	90
219-Meditation	90
220-Meditation	91
221-Meditation	91
222-Meditation	91
223-Meditation	91
224-Meditation	92
225-Meditation	92
226-Meditation	92
227-Meditation	92
228-Meditation	92
229-Meditation	93
230-Meditation	93
231-Meditation	93
232-Meditation	93
233-Meditation	93
234-Meditation	94
235-Meditation	94
236-Meditation	94
237-Meditation	95
238-Meditation	95
239-Meditation	95
240-Meditation	95
241-Meditation	95
242-Meditation	96
243-Meditation	96
244-Meditation	97
245-Meditation	97
246-Meditation	97
247-Meditation	97
248-Meditation	98

The Council Of Living Saints
The Meditations Of A Christian Saint

249-Meditation 98
250-Meditation 98
251-Meditation 98
252-Meditation 99
253-Meditation 99
254-Meditation 99
255-Meditation 99
256-Meditation 99
257-Meditation 100
258-Meditation 100
259-Meditation 100
260-Meditation 100
261-Meditation 101
262-Meditation 101
263-Meditation 101
264-Meditation 101
265-Meditation 101
266-Meditation 102
267-Meditation 102
268-Meditation 102
269-Meditation 102
270-Meditation 102
271-Meditation 103
272-Meditation 103
273-Meditation 103
274-Meditation 103
275-Meditation 104
276-Meditation 104
277-Meditation 104
278-Meditation 104
279-Meditation 105
280-Meditation 105
281-Meditation 105
282-Meditation 105
283-Meditation 105
284-Meditation 106
285-Meditation 106
286-Meditation 106
287-Meditation 106
288-Meditation 107
289-Meditation 108

290-Meditation 108
291-Meditation 108
292-Meditation 108
293-Meditation 109
294-Meditation 109
295-Meditation 110
296-Meditation 110
297-Meditation 111
298-Meditation 111
299-Meditation 111
300-Meditation 112

The Council Of Living Saints
The Meditations Of A Christian Saint

ACKNOWLEDGMENTS

This book has been a labor of love and faith, and its completion would not have been possible without the support, encouragement, and inspiration of many remarkable individuals. To each of you, I extend my heartfelt gratitude:

I acknowledge GOD's divine presence in my life and grace that has illuminated the path of my spiritual journey and guided my thoughts as I penned these pages.

I write with the hope that these meditations of Christian a Saint may bring you comfort, inspiration, and a deeper purpose and connection to your faith. Thank you for embarking on this journey with me.

With sincere gratitude,

Agyeman Bonsu

The Council Of Living Saints
The Meditations Of A Christian Saint

Introduction

Within the pages of "The Council of Living Saints: The Meditations of A Christian Saint," we embark on a profound exploration of the multifaceted essence of Saints—a journey that traverses the realms of religion, philosophy, and metaphysics. They span cultures, religions, and civilizations, leaving an indelible mark on the spiritual landscapes of humanity. Saints, in their transcendent state, transcend the limitations of mortal existence, becoming conduits of divine grace and wisdom. Regardless of whether we encounter them in the context of Christianity, Islam, Buddhism, Hinduism, or other spiritual traditions, Saints universally command reverence, devotion, and admiration. They serve as beacons of inspiration for seekers of truth and spiritual enlightenment, having ascended to heights of divine communion that illuminate the path for humanity.

At their core, Saints understand the vulnerabilities of humans on Earth, recognizing the fundamental law of survival that all lives should thrive without harming another. They abide by the law of love, tirelessly protecting the vulnerable, defending the weak, and often sacrificing their own well-being for the greater good. Their lives are testimonies to benevolence, self-sacrifice, and an unwavering commitment to a higher purpose. In their devotion to a divine force or higher power, Saints pave the way for others to explore profound truths about existence, the cosmos, and the enigmatic realm of metaphysics. Saints are not mere historical figures or revered personalities; they symbolize the universal human aspiration to transcend the mundane, the selfish, and the materialistic world to seek deeper meaning and forge an intimate connection with the divine or ultimate reality. Their lives and teachings are reservoirs of spiritual knowledge, inspiring countless souls on their quests for self-discovery and divine realization.

While the concept of a Saint may vary across religious and philosophical spectra, one unifying thread emerges—the unwavering commitment to a life of profound compassion, selflessness, and humility. Whether through the ascetic practices of an Eastern mystic, the virtuous deeds of a Western martyr, or the philosophical insights of a sage, the lives of Saints beckon us to reflect on our own existence and the deeper purpose that unites us all.

As we contemplate the lives of Saints, we must also acknowledge the inherent complexities and paradoxes within their journeys. They, too, grappled with doubts, fears, and inner conflicts, making their quest for divine realization a deeply human pursuit. Together, we shall explore the intersection of their divine experiences with the tangible world, witnessing how their teachings have shaped societies and cultures, fostering an enduring legacy that resonates with humanity even today.

In our exploration of the lives of these remarkable individuals, we invite you to open your heart and mind to the profound lessons they offer. Let us journey together into the depths of wisdom, seeking to unlock the eternal truths that illuminate our paths toward transcendence and spiritual enlightenment. It is important to recognize that the concept of sanctity may carry unique meanings within different religions or societies, but at its core, it represents a profound commitment to the welfare of others and an intimate connection with the divine. As we delve into the lives and meditations of Saints, we enter into a world where selflessness and empathy reign supreme. Saints demonstrate an unyielding dedication to the welfare and progress of others, often at the expense of their own needs and desires. Their actions are guided by a deep understanding of the interconnectedness of all life, recognizing the intrinsic value and sanctity of every living being.

The Council Of Living Saints
The Meditations Of A Christian Saint

Patriotism, within the context of Saints, extends beyond mere nationalistic loyalty. They exhibit a profound love and devotion to their fellow beings and the broader community in which they reside. Their sense of duty towards their country or community is deeply rooted in a genuine desire to uplift and enhance the lives of others, regardless of their backgrounds or affiliations.

Saints also share a remarkable affinity with nature, perceiving the environment as a manifestation of the divine and treating it with reverence and care. Their actions reflect a harmonious relationship with nature, recognizing its intrinsic value and the interconnectedness of all living beings within the ecosystem.

While Saints' expressions of spirituality and their understanding of the divine (GOD) may vary across religious and philosophical traditions, they all share an intimate connection with the transcendent. Their spiritual journey is marked by a profound communion with the sacred, often leading to insights and experiences that inspire them to embody virtues like love, compassion, forgiveness, and humility.

In the lives of Saints, we often find a transformative power that stems from their ability to transcend their individual ego and align themselves with a higher purpose. They inspire others to follow in their footsteps, fostering a ripple effect of positive change and moral elevation in society.

Ultimately, a Saint is not a flawless individual, but one who, despite their human imperfections, strives relentlessly to embody and manifest the divine qualities of love, selflessness, and compassion. Their legacy serves as an eternal source of inspiration, reminding us of the limitless potential for goodness and service that resides within each human heart. Their profound impact on the world and their enduring influence on subsequent generations demonstrate the enduring power of a life dedicated to seeking the advancement, advantage, and development of others, nature, and a deeper connection with the divine (GOD).

Who is a Saint?

A Saint, in the traditional sense, has often been associated with holy figures recognized by religious institutions after their death for their exceptional piety and virtuous deeds.

According to the Council of the Living Saints, CLS, Saints are not solely figures from the past, but living individuals who, across all races, religions, cultures, and nations, walk among us, embodying the principles of selflessness, compassion, and devotion to the welfare of others, nature, and the divine. CLS acknowledges that Saintliness is not confined to specific religious traditions or historical periods but is a timeless and universal virtue that can be found in people from all walks of life. Living Saints, through their actions and character, inspire and uplift others, serving as beacons of light and love in an often turbulent world.

A Saint, as defined in the context of the two laws of life, embodies the fundamental principles of Survival and Love (representing God or Life itself). These laws are intertwined and shape the Saint's character, actions, and devotion to serving others and the greater good.

The law of Survival emphasizes the innate drive of all life to live and grow. It recognizes that life is a precious gift that seeks to flourish and evolve. CLS acknowledges that life is the breadth and spark of GOD, the one source of all things, in every living form. As such, indeed it is only a fool that lives and says there is no GOD, for his or her very life is God. A Saint, deeply attuned to this law, cherishes and respects all forms of life, recognizing the interconnectedness and interdependence of every living being. They strive to preserve and nurture life in all its forms, be it humans, animals, the creatures, or the natural world.

Conversely, the law of Love/God/Life promotes selflessness and interconnectedness. It calls upon individuals to embrace a higher level of consciousness that transcends selfish desires and ego-driven pursuits. Saints acknowledge the priceless value of life as invested by GOD in His creatures offering each world that respect and promotes the full expression of this life and godliness. In adhering to this law, Saints embody a profound sense of compassion and empathy towards others, placing the welfare of others before their own.

The law of Love/God/Life is manifested in the Saint's commitment to not take life or exploit resources at the expense of others. Saints recognize that their existence and well-being are intrinsically linked to the well-being of all creation. As such, they approach life with humility and reverence, seeking to live in harmony with nature and other beings.

Love, in the Saint's understanding, goes beyond mere sentimentality; it is an active force that motivates them to serve and uplift others. Through selfless service, Saints express their love for humanity and the divine, seeking to enrich the lives of those they encounter. Their actions are driven by a genuine desire to help others live and grow, even if it means sacrificing their comfort or resources.

A Saint's life becomes a testament to the depth of love they embody. They not only share their wisdom and knowledge but also their material resources and essentials, understanding that true fulfillment lies in giving and sharing rather than amassing and hoarding. Their service to others is fueled by a profound understanding of the interconnectedness of life, where everyone's well-being is intimately linked to the well-being of others.

Patriotism, in the context of Saints, refers to their profound love and devotion to their homeland, culture, and community. Patriotism transcends mere loyalty to a nation or a specific group; it expands to encompass a profound love and care for all of humanity. A Saint's patriotism is not limited to political borders but extends to a broader understanding of humanity as a global family.

Saints exemplify a universal outlook, recognizing the interconnectedness of all life forms and fostering a sense of global kinship. Their love for humanity is boundless, extending even to those who may oppose or persecute them. They are driven by a genuine sense of duty and responsibility toward the betterment of their society and nation.

A Saint is a remarkable individual who embodies a unique combination of spiritual virtues, selflessness, and unwavering commitment to the welfare and development of others, nature, and a higher power, often referred to as God or the divine. Such individuals rise above the ordinary and exemplify the highest ideals of humanity, serving as beacons of light and moral exemplars for their communities and the world at large.

At the core of a Saint's character lies a deep sense of selflessness and compassion. They genuinely care for the well-being of others and willingly dedicate their lives to alleviating the suffering and challenges faced by their fellow beings. Saints possess an innate desire to uplift and advance the lives of those around them, often at great personal sacrifice.

A distinguishing hallmark of Saints is their deep connection to nature and their recognition of its sacredness. They view the natural world as an expression of divine beauty and wisdom, deserving of respect, preservation, and harmony. In their reverence for nature, Saints strive to protect the environment and promote sustainable practices, recognizing the interconnectedness of all living beings.

Central to the identity of a Saint is their profound relationship with GOD, the Ultimate Reality, or Divine, a higher power, whom they perceive as the ultimate source of love, wisdom, and truth. While their understanding of GOD may vary based on their religious or spiritual tradition, Saints share an intimate communion with the divine. This relationship often forms the bedrock of their spiritual journey, guiding their actions and decisions with a sense of divine purpose. Saints find solace and strength in prayer, meditation, or other forms of spiritual practice, seeking to deepen their connection with the divine and align their lives with higher principles.

Through their exemplary lives, Saints become beacons of hope and inspiration for those seeking spiritual guidance and meaning. They offer a path for others to follow, characterized by selfless service, love, and reverence for all creation. Saints' actions are not motivated by personal gain or recognition but are driven by an authentic desire to be instruments of divine grace and agents of positive change in the world.

In essence, a Saint represents the epitome of human potential, demonstrating the capacity to transcend the ego and embrace a higher purpose that encompasses the welfare of all beings, the preservation of nature, and a deep spiritual connection with the divine. Their lives stand as living testimonies to the profound impact an individual can have on the world when guided by selflessness, compassion, and unwavering devotion to the advancement and betterment of all aspects of creation.

At the heart of a Saint's character lies an unwavering commitment to selflessness. They embody the essence of compassion and empathy, dedicating their lives to alleviating the suffering of fellow beings and uplifting those in need. Driven by an innate desire to see others flourish, Saints selflessly devote their time, energy, and resources to serve the greater good. Seeking the advancement, advantage, and development of others, Saints become agents of positive change. They work tirelessly to empower individuals, communities, and societies, aiming to uplift and foster growth in all aspects of life. By embodying values such as justice, equality, and inclusivity, they become catalysts for transformation and progress.

Moreover, Saints demonstrate an intimate connection with nature. Their reverence for the natural world extends beyond environmental stewardship; it becomes a spiritual communion with the divine essence present in all creation. They see the interconnectedness of the universe, recognizing the divine handiwork in every living being and natural phenomenon.

At the core of a Saint's life is their profound relationship with God, the Ultimate Reality, or the Divine. While their understanding of God may vary based on their religious or spiritual tradition, Saints share an intimate communion with the divine. Their spiritual journey becomes a ceaseless pursuit of truth, enlightenment, and unity with the transcendent source.

In conclusion, a Saint is an exceptional individual who embodies the virtues of selflessness, compassion, and love for humanity, working tirelessly for the advancement and development of others, nature, and their profound connection with God. Their lives serve as shining examples of the boundless potential within every human being to transcend the ordinary and embrace the extraordinary in the service of the greater good. Saints leave an indelible mark on the fabric of human history, inspiring generations to come and reminding us of the innate nobility of the human spirit.

CHAPTER 1
A Christian Saint

In the Bible, particularly in the New Testament, believers in Jesus Christ were referred to as Saints. The term "Saints" appears numerous times in the Bible, demonstrating its

significance as a central concept in Christian theology. Though the exact number may vary depending on the translation and version of the Bible, the term "Saints" is mentioned over 60 times in the New Testament alone, highlighting the emphasis placed on the sanctity and holiness of believers in Christ.

On the other hand, the term "Christian" is mentioned relatively few times in the Bible, appearing only three times in the New Testament. This term, coined in Antioch (Acts 11:26), initially referred to followers of Jesus Christ and has since become the widely recognized term for those who adhere to the Christian faith. The 'Christian' Saints believe that;

- Man is created lower than angels but has power in Christ to attain the fullness of the GOD.

- Man falls together with the creation from grace and glory and limits the manifestation of GOD in them. Satan, the prince of this world took dominion from man and ruled since the 'beginning' of earth by devils.

- Imagining time as a number line where zero to negative is infinity, represents past consciousness and the opposite end, the future. GOD is outside of all times for he has no infinity nor can man fathom in his mind the beginning of all beginnings within the negative infinity of time. The start of any event, creation, or occurrence in the universe is called the beginning, the beginning of a new consciousness, the record but not the foundations of the cosmic universe or GOD, and the beginning of all times. So, Genesis is a beginning but not the beginning of all beginnings. Revelation talks about the beginning. The reset of reality and life is what is normally called in modern terms New World Order where the past is lost, forgotten, masked, erased for the current consciousness, or rewritten to make way for the new order.

- Man, knowingly or unknowingly, believing or not believing wrestles with the serpent and its seed, fallen angels and their seeds, other creatures (beings), and currently the robots in the age of AI. Unlike GOD who is all 'powerful' than His creation, man (if so, it was) has created AI to be not only a helper but, a god in AI. The concern is that there are devils who will use AI as before to steal, kill, and destroy lives. There is nothing new under the sun.

- GOD waited after Abel for Seth who was anointed unto GOD and after the image and likeness of Adam. The spiritual battle of the seed of Cain, devils, creatures, and the seed of Seth has been ongoing since the fall in Eden. The seed of fallen angels and the serpent according to

Genesis were more intelligent, renowned, giants (in size and mind). Their deeds were evil and the devilish such that they made man evil and caused GOD to destroy them and the world with water in the days of Noah. Yet the fallen angels continue to walk the earth after the flood.

- Humans have vulnerabilities as discussed in the coming chapters which gives the devils the advantage over man such that they enslaved the earth. Though a man has the will to choose, there is no choice without options to choose from. Thus the one that provides or controls the options of choice inadvertently limits or controls the will. The battle of GOOD and Evil between Saints and devils continues until the final battle when Jesus Christ, GOD, and the Saints will end it all.

- With Power and influence man is what you make them. A child is born into a world with already established laws, systems, cultures, and other influences. As a person becomes what he thinks, if the fountain of thought is tinted or corrupted or the faculty brewing thoughts into ideas is destroyed, such a man is nothing but the product of him that controls him. As one grows experiences and beliefs, conditions, shapes the attitude, and personality in life. Devils have done intense studies on man and can use all tools to deceive and influence man. Who else will deliver, protect, and defend man but the Saints?

The Council Of Living Saints
The Meditations Of A Christian Saint

- As Saints have the spirit of Christ so has a devil the spirit of Satan. We wrestle not [only] against flesh and blood, but ... In that as God, Jesus Christ works or manifests through man, angels, and creatures on earth so does Satan work by man, the devil, demons, and the creature. We use 'the creatures' for all other beings that walk the earth yet unknown or description is beyond the scope of this book. For we are not all humans nor are we alone.

- A devil is a person, the creature, or spirit that steals, kills, and destroys life. A devil is also one that makes devils out of man. Devils manifest evil. Jesus said not 12 have I chosen, and one is a devil.

- Christian Saints believe that there is a law of sin and death that operates in man and nature making man subject to the influence of the devil. For the good a man wants to do he cannot but the evil he does not want that he does. Yet thank GOD for Christ, that by faith and the way of Christ, another law is given, the law of the Spirit of Christ that motives or vitalizes the mortal body to live unto righteousness, love, Saintliness, and godliness. In Christ and Christ alone can a person escape the fallen nature of the creation and rise above instinct to survive or overcome the fear of death. It is by the Spirit of Christ that a Saint can fight the good fight of faith, against demons, devils, and the creatures that work evil. For Christ was revealed to destroy the works of the enemy.

In conclusion, living Saints, according to the Council of Living Saints, are individuals from diverse backgrounds who embody the virtues of selflessness, love, and devotion to the well-being of others, nature, and the divine. The Council of Living Saints embodies and highlights the universality of Saintliness and the potential for Saint-like qualities to be manifested by people across the globe, transcending barriers of race, religion, culture, or nationality. Additionally, the term "Saints" is mentioned numerous times in the Bible, particularly in the New Testament, emphasizing the importance of sanctity and holiness among believers in Jesus Christ.

CHAPTER 2
The Character of a Saint

A Saint is an exceptional individual who embodies a unique combination of virtues, qualities, and characteristics that transcend ordinary human experience. While the concept

of a Saint can vary across different religious, philosophical, and cultural contexts, certain common threads weave through their definition. A Saint is typically characterized by:

Moral Exemplarship: Saints are paragons of virtue and moral excellence. They consistently demonstrate a deep commitment to ethical principles such as compassion, kindness, humility, and selflessness. Their actions and decisions are guided by a profound sense of rightness and an unwavering dedication to upholding the highest standards of moral conduct.

Selflessness and Service: Saints are driven by a selfless and genuine concern for the well-being of others. Their lives are marked by acts of charity, benevolence, and a relentless dedication to serving the needs of their fellow human beings. Their altruism extends beyond personal gain, as they derive true fulfillment from uplifting and assisting others.

Spiritual Devotion: Saints often share a profound and intimate connection with the divine or spiritual realm. Whether through prayer, meditation, or other forms of communion with the sacred, they cultivate a deep and unwavering relationship with a higher power or a transcendent reality. This spiritual connection serves as a wellspring of inspiration for their actions and beliefs.

Advancement and Enlightenment: Saints are driven by an insatiable thirst for knowledge, wisdom, and enlightenment. They constantly seek to understand the deeper truths of existence, the nature of reality, and the mysteries of the universe. Their pursuit of knowledge is not solely for personal gain, but rather to share their insights and guidance with others.

Patriotism and Advocacy: Saints also exhibit a fervent love and dedication to their homeland, culture, or community. They may champion causes related to social justice, human rights, or the advancement of their nation. Their patriotism is often intertwined with their commitment to the welfare and progress of all beings.

Harmony with Nature: Saints often display a profound reverence and respect for the natural world. They recognize the interconnectedness of all life forms and advocate for the responsible stewardship of the environment. Their relationship with nature reflects their holistic understanding of existence and their role within the grand tapestry of creation.

Miracles and Divine Manifestations: In many traditions, Saints are attributed with performing miracles or divine interventions. These extraordinary occurrences are often seen as manifestations of the Saint's close alignment with the divine and their ability to channel divine power for the betterment of others.

CHAPTER 3

Embracing the Identity of a Living Saint Implications

Choosing to live as a Saint in the present, as opposed to the notion of achieving Sainthood only afterlife holds profound implications across various dimensions of human experience: psychological, emotional, conscious, and theological. This decision transcends religious confines, encompassing a broader understanding of virtuous living and spiritual devotion.

Let's explore each aspect:

Psychological Impact: Accepting oneself as a Saint and living as such can have a positive psychological impact. The realization that one is called to embody the qualities of love, compassion, and selflessness can bring a sense of purpose and fulfillment. This newfound purpose can act as a guiding force, providing a clear moral compass for decision-making and actions. Embracing Saintliness may also foster resilience in the face of challenges, as the individual is driven by a higher calling and a sense of divine support. The perception of being a Saint can foster a strong sense of purpose, meaning, and self-worth. It can imbue individuals with a deep sense of inner strength and resilience, as they align their lives with the noble virtues and principles associated with Sainthood. Identifying oneself as a living Saint and consciously living up to that standard can have a transformative effect on one's psychology. This self-perception cultivates a sense of purpose, direction, and moral clarity. It fosters a deepened self-awareness and encourages the individual to align their thoughts, actions, and intentions with the highest ideals of compassion, selflessness, and service. This shift in mindset can lead to greater mental well-being, a sense of fulfillment, and a reduction in inner conflicts, as the individual strives to live consistently with their chosen identity.

This self-identification as a Saint may also lead to increased self-awareness and introspection. The process of introspection can encourage individuals to examine their thoughts, emotions, and behaviors, fostering personal growth and spiritual development.

Emotional Impact: Emotionally, accepting the identity of being a Saint and striving to live up to that standard can cultivate a profound sense of compassion and empathy toward others. This emotional transformation allows individuals to be more open-hearted, understanding, and forgiving, fostering harmonious relationships and deeper connections with fellow human beings. Living as a Saint entails a profound emotional journey. The commitment to selflessness and service opens the heart to empathy, compassion, and love for all beings. This deep connection to others and the world at large can bring about a heightened sense of emotional well-being, as the individual's focus shifts from self-centered concerns to the well-being of others. Acts of kindness, generosity, and love become natural expressions of their character, nurturing a sense of joy and contentment that arises from making a positive impact on the lives of others.

The emotional impact of living as a Saint may also lead to a greater sense of inner peace and contentment. The act of selfless service and devoting oneself to the welfare of others can bring joy, fulfillment, and a sense of purpose that transcends personal desires and ego-driven pursuits.

Conscious Impact: Living as a Saint requires a heightened level of consciousness and mindfulness. This conscious impact is marked by a heightened awareness of one's thoughts, actions, and intentions. Aspiring to embody the virtues associated with Sainthood necessitates a constant examination of one's choices and behavior in alignment with the principles of love, compassion, and service. Consciously choosing to live as a Saint involves a continuous process of self-reflection and self-improvement. The individual becomes attuned to their thoughts, emotions, and actions, seeking to refine their character and align themselves with the principles of their chosen path. This heightened consciousness encourages mindfulness, ethical decision-making, and a commitment to personal growth. By fostering a sense of inner harmony and integrity, this conscious approach to life facilitates a deeper connection to one's own spirituality and the world around them.

Through this conscious living, individuals may experience a deeper connection to the present moment, fostering a sense of gratitude for the beauty and wonders of life. Such a heightened consciousness can lead to a more profound spiritual experience and a sense of interconnectedness with all living beings and nature.

Theological Impact: The theological impact of accepting oneself as a Saint and living accordingly is rooted in the understanding of one's divine potential and inherent connection with the divine. From a theological perspective, embracing the identity of a Saint acknowledges the inherent divinity within each individual and affirms the idea that all human beings are capable of manifesting divine qualities in their lives. The theological implications of embracing the identity of a living Saint extend beyond religious dogma. It reflects a profound understanding of the interconnectedness of all life and the inherent divinity that resides within each being. This perspective aligns with the teachings of various spiritual traditions that emphasize love, service, and the pursuit of higher truths. From a theological standpoint, choosing to live as a Saint affirms the belief in the potential for spiritual transformation and enlightenment within the realm of human experience.

Living as a Saint in the present life aligns with the notion of seeking the "kingdom of God" or spiritual enlightenment in the here and now, rather than deferring it to the afterlife. This theological perspective emphasizes the transformational power of living a life of love, service, and selflessness in creating a more spiritually fulfilling and meaningful existence.

Living up to a Higher Standard: Living as a Saint challenges individuals to hold themselves to a higher standard of moral conduct and spiritual practice. Embodying the qualities of a Saint means consistently striving to live in alignment with the principles of love, compassion, and selflessness. This commitment to a higher standard can act as a catalyst for personal growth and self-improvement, as individuals continuously seek to overcome their own limitations and evolve spiritually.

Living as a Saint can lead to a life of profound significance and impact. The actions and teachings of Saints throughout history have inspired generations, transforming societies, and influencing the course of history. Embracing Saintliness in everyday life allows individuals to leave a lasting legacy of goodness and positive change. Such a life becomes a shining example of the transformative power of love and service, influencing others to follow a similar path of compassion and spiritual devotion.

In contrast, the traditional notion of becoming a Saint after one's death, often associated with Christian teachings, emphasizes posthumous recognition. While this belief can provide comfort and hope, choosing to embody Saintliness in the present can be seen as a more proactive and dynamic approach to spirituality. It empowers individuals to make a tangible difference in the world, promote positive change, and contribute to the greater good during their lifetime. Embracing the identity of a Saint and living according to the principles of Saintliness can lead to transformative psychological, emotional, conscious, and theological effects. It challenges individuals to rise above their ego-driven desires, embrace a higher standard of living, and commit to a life of selfless service and compassion. By adopting this perspective, individuals can experience a deepened sense of purpose, emotional fulfillment, self-awareness, and a profound connection to the divine within themselves and all of creation. It empowers individuals to live with purpose, compassion, and mindfulness, fostering a deeper connection to oneself, others, and the divine. By striving to be a Saint in the present life, individuals can find a higher standard of living that transcends personal aspirations and contributes to a more compassionate and harmonious world.

CHAPTER 4
Council of Living Saints

The Council of the Living Saints is a transformative and visionary society that embodies the profound ideals of Saintliness, recognizing the sacredness of every land and

the divine providence that sustains all life. The Council of the Living Saints is a beacon of light in a world yearning for compassion, unity, and divine purpose. This assembly of individuals, hailing from diverse backgrounds, cultures, and faiths, embodies the sacred fusion of Saintliness and patriotism, illuminating the profound connection between love for one's land and devotion to a higher power. United by their shared commitment to selflessness, love, and service, the Saints within this organization are also patriots who hold a deep reverence for their homeland and people.

In the eyes of a Saint, every land is abundantly blessed by the very essence of life – God's divine life force – providing all that is needed for sustenance, growth, and godliness. No corner of this Earth is barren of the divine providence needed for life, growth, and godliness. Such understanding empowers Saints to ensure that their people enjoy the abundant fruits of the land, seeking the prosperity and well-being of their communities without discrimination or exclusion. The Council recognizes that a Saint's role encompasses not only selfless service to their people but also a sacred duty to ensure that the blessings of the land are shared equitably among all. Saints are indeed patriots, champions of their homeland's prosperity, and custodians of its resources. Their selflessness extends beyond individual concerns to safeguard the well-being of their people, ensuring that the abundant gifts of the land are nurtured and shared. A Saint's commitment to their people's flourishing is unwavering, a testament to the belief that each life is a sacred trust to be nurtured and cherished.

However, a Saint's devotion to their people and homeland does not come at the expense of disregarding the sovereignty of other lives and lands. Embodying the belief that all life emanates from the same divine source, Saints view humanity as one global family under the care of a loving and benevolent Creator. This realization fosters a sense of unity and interconnectedness, inspiring Saints to respect and cherish all lives, regardless of nationality, culture, or background.

While upholding the sanctity of all life, a Saint also stands as a protector, defending against forces that threaten the well-being and growth of their people. These adversaries, known as "Devils," can take the form of external or domestic enemies or challenges that hinder the progress of society. A Saint courageously confronts these obstacles, striving to preserve and promote the flourishing of life in all its forms.

In the pursuit of justice and protection of life, Saints stand united as defenders of both land and spirit. Their actions transcend geographical boundaries, acknowledging that the fight against darkness knows no borders. This courageous stance is a testament to the unwavering commitment to uphold the divine principle that all lives must live, and that the light of existence must prevail overshadows.

With unwavering love and compassion, the Council of the Living Saints champions the cause of humanity and the environment. By recognizing the divine unity that binds us all, they extend a hand of friendship and cooperation to others, seeking collaboration across borders and cultures. As true patriots, they work tirelessly to foster harmony and prosperity within their homeland while respecting the dignity and sovereignty of other nations.

Through their exemplary lives and noble actions, the Saints in the Council inspire countless others to embrace the path of selfless service and embrace the truth that "WE THE PEOPLE ARE ONE FROM ONE GOD." They stand as living examples of how love, understanding, and compassion can bridge divides and transform the world into a harmonious and godly abode for all living beings.

In this ever-changing world, the Council of the Living Saints stands as a beacon of hope, a testament to the transformative power of divine love, and a catalyst for positive change. With their unwavering commitment to the well-being of all, they pave the way toward a future where humanity embraces its shared heritage, protecting and cherishing life in all its diverse and magnificent manifestations. The Council of the Living Saints shines as a testament to the harmonious symphony of faith, patriotism, compassion, and divine devotion. Their collective presence stands as a living embodiment of unity, an eloquent proclamation that love for one's land and reverence for all life are harmonious threads woven into the grand tapestry of existence. With each selfless act, and each gesture of compassion, the Council affirms the boundless potential for greatness within humanity – a potential that springs from the very heart of GOD, the eternal wellspring of life, growth, and godliness.

CHAPTER 5

The Human Fallen State or Condition: Vulnerabilities and Weaknesses

Humanity stands as a complex and intricate thread, woven with strengths, aspirations, and dreams. Yet, as we delve deeper into the fabric of human existence, we must also acknowledge Strengths, Weaknesses, Opportunities, and Threats, SWOT analysis of the vulnerabilities and weaknesses that are part and parcel of this intricate design.

Mortality, the undeniable specter that hovers over the entirety of human existence, exerts an unassailable influence. Over time, it becomes increasingly apparent that the human lifespan exhibits a perpetual descent. Presently, the average span of active living stands at a mere 70 years, with the initial two decades dedicated to growth and self-discovery, and the final two decades to inevitable decline, introspection, and contemplation of life's conclusion. This leaves us with a critical 30-year period of vitality and purpose, contingent, naturally, on how we navigate the bookends of our existence- those initial and concluding twenty years. This latent dread of mortality stealthily goads humanity into fear and relentless pursuit of ephemeral moments of joy, a quest for meaning, and the creation of legacies intended to transcend the inescapable grip of death. Paradoxically, it is within this vulnerability that the crucible of courage and resilience is forged.

Emotions, the vivid colors that paint the human experience, are a double-edged sword. They bestow the capacity to love, empathize, and forge profound connections. Yet, emotions can also be turbulent seas, causing doubt, anger, and despair. Vulnerable to their own feelings, humans navigate these emotional waters, sometimes becoming ensnared in their depths.

Emotions are powerful human experiences, expressions, and assets that if one doesn't intelligently control can be destructive or weaponized against the individual.

Physical limitations of humanity are a testament to both fragility and strength. A broken bone mends, a heart heals, but the scars remain, a testament to past vulnerabilities. These bodies, fragile and resilient, house the essence of humanity, bearing the marks of countless struggles and triumphs. Disease susceptibility, the ultimate vulnerability, reminds humanity of its shared mortality. The capacity to heal and endure through countless plagues and pandemics reveals the indomitable spirit residing within the human soul.

Need for needs. The very core of human existence is intertwined with dependency on basic needs. Food, water, shelter, and sleep are the cornerstones of survival, and any disruption in their provision exposes the delicate balance upon which humans teeter. Vulnerable in the face of scarcity, humans strive to secure these essentials for themselves and their kin. The quest and instinct to survive, for the fear of death, the suffering of needs, and lack can lead to selfishness, greed, and lust among other sins. The lack therefore seems to influence many aspects if not all our lives. As individuals coming to the earth, we are met with already established systems of resource distribution, governance, religions, norms, cultures, and others that affect our attainment of basic needs of life. However, the organization of people into families is the core of every nation and country, providing resources needed to live by the efforts of many. As a citizen of the land, you then obtain benefits just like any other everywhere on land.

Limited knowledge is a chink in the armor of humanity. Generally, a person is born without knowledge of self or the environment. Coupled with forgetfulness and limiting retainage ability, people tend to know from the environment rather than from within thus susceptible to disinformation and misinformation. Wherein acquisition of information is the bedrock of knowledge, upon which understanding is built for wisdom to live in. All that there is of yesterday is but a dream to remember as if the past was only yesterday. The fountain of ethers of thought of a person can be poisoned or corrupted leaving the springs of ideas and imaginations to the screening and forging capacity of the reasoning faculty. In the forging process of thoughts, one may lack the ability to focus, track, and suspend multiple thoughts at the same time or even a single thought for a long time. There exists opportunity cost in the thought realm as such distraction is a sad vulnerability of man so much so that most live off autopiloting unknowingly. A person understands his thoughts in words that are limited by the language he uses. That is, the use of words wrongly assigned to meaning can influence the sense one makes of his thoughts. Individual understanding is but a drop in the vast ocean of wisdom that surrounds them. It is a vulnerability that exposes them to the allure of misinformation and manipulation.

The tensile, elastic, and malleable but not too ductile nature of the mind are psychological vulnerabilities. Stress, anxiety, and mental health challenges cast long shadows. Yet, it is these very shadows that can lead individuals to unearth inner strength, forging resilience in the crucible of adversity.

The Unseen Identity

A man is still the man if he loses his feet,
Despite the change, his essence remains fleet,
For limbs are but vessels, not the core,
The spirit within still forevermore.

The man is still the man if he becomes lamed,
The fire in his soul can never be tamed,
Though steps may falter, strength resides,
In the heart that beats, where true self abides.

The man is still the man if his limbs are lost,
The body may change, but identity is embossed,
Beyond the surface, beyond the skin,
A soul unshaken, a light from within.

The man is still the man without the body's base,
From abdomen to toes, a new kind of space,
The vessel transforms, yet the essence prevails,
A unique story, a self that unveils.

A man is still the man even without speech,
For words may falter, but truths still reach,
In the silence that follows, a deeper connection,
A spirit unbounded, seeking introspection.

The Council Of Living Saints
The Meditations Of A Christian Saint

The man is still the man even without sight,
Though darkness surrounds, there's still inner light,
In blindness, a new vision, a perspective refined,

But who is he without the guiding mind?
For who is he that has lost his MIND,
A puzzle unsolved, a question unmined,
He may show up, a shadow, a guise,
A stranger within, where the confusion lies.

And who is the MIND without the Spirit? Such a person, being or thing is intelligent but disconnected from the universal source of life.

Social influence weaves a complex web around every human, for they are creatures molded by society's norms, customs, and expectations. The whole society is based on trust, the world runs on trust in the systems, institutions, and governments around the world at the free will of people. This trust is inculcated and instilled in everyone from birth. The vulnerability to conform, to please, and to be accepted is both a source of strength in unity and a weakness when it stifles individuality.

Ethical dilemmas, the moral crossroads of human existence, often bear the weight of difficult decisions. The vulnerability to err in the pursuit of one's principles is a testament to the ceaseless quest for justice and virtue.

In the age of technological dependence, humanity's creations have become both a boon and a bane. The vulnerability of interconnected systems reveals itself when technology falters, raising questions about the price of progress. A more recent but not so new is the threat of AI to humans and the universe. AI is good with immersive potential to better lives but created or in the hands of an evil entity (Devil) can spell doom for all. Unlike GOD who created man, AI can be more powerful and independent of its creator.

Alteration of physical Makeup. Man is a Spirit with a soul and lives in a body. The body is a mortal, organic, and complex machine that houses the Spirit of Man. This body that can limit the manifestation of the spirit can be changed genetically by spiritual or laboratory experimentation, radiation, food (ingestions), and evolution (adaptation and environmental changes).

In light of the myriad weaknesses inherent or accompanying the human condition, the Council of Living Saints steadfastly strives and upholds its mission to the preservation, guardianship, inspiration, salvation, transcendence, and fortification of humanity and the intricate web of life that sustains us.

Acknowledging the fragility of our existence, inherent and artificial limitations, and creature-created world this dedicated institution strives to provide comprehensive protection, addressing not only physical vulnerabilities but also the profound emotional and spiritual dimensions of our shared humanity.

The Council's mission extends beyond mere physical protection. They serve as beacons of emotional and spiritual sustenance, recognizing that humans are not only physical entities but also spiritual beings seeking meaning and purpose in the face of their vulnerabilities.

The Council Of Living Saints
The Meditations Of A Christian Saint

Moreover, as stewards of the Earth's environment, the Council of Living Saints champions environmental sustainability, embracing the profound interconnectedness of humanity and the planet. In the face of the vulnerabilities we inherit, they work tirelessly to ensure the legacy they craft is one of balance, preservation, and the perpetual coexistence of generations.

These vulnerabilities are not blemishes to be hidden away but rather crucibles from which courage and resilience emerge. It is within this profound recognition of human frailty that the Council draws its strength and purpose, unyielding in its resolve to protect and sustain both humanity and the intricate web of life, all the while understanding that it is within these very vulnerabilities that our true potential and resilience are forged."

CHAPTER 6
Overcoming individual weaknesses

Rising above weaknesses and mitigating vulnerabilities is a journey of personal growth and self-improvement. While humans may never eliminate their vulnerabilities, they can take steps to strengthen themselves and develop strategies to navigate life more effectively. Here are some ways individuals can rise above their weaknesses or mitigate their vulnerabilities:

Self-awareness: Recognizing these and one's weaknesses is the first step to mitigating them. Self-awareness allows individuals to acknowledge their vulnerabilities, know the enemies within and without, enemies of their souls, bodies, and spirits, understand how they impact their lives, and master defensive mechanisms.

Education and Knowledge: "My people are destroyed for lack of knowledge: because thou hast rejected knowledge, I will also reject thee, that thou shalt be no priest to me: seeing thou hast forgotten the law of thy God, I will also forget thy children" Hosea 4:6 King James Version (KJV). To combat limited knowledge, individuals can invest in education and continuous learning. There is knowledge unto survival in the world and the knowledge unto salvation. "And this is life eternal, that they might know thee the only true God, and Jesus Christ, whom thou hast sent." John 17:3. There are levels of meaning, superficial to ocean deep is a word of knowledge. One's knowledge must transcend merely acknowledging and remembering a fact to understanding the fact and then applying the fact in life. Expanding one's knowledge base and critical thinking skills can help in making informed decisions and resisting manipulation. Financial Literacy is a must your access to and power to acquire resources and necessities of life depends on it. Learn about money management, budgeting, wealth creation, and investing. Make informed financial decisions to secure your future.

Emotional Intelligence: Emotions are subject to manipulations and triggers both internally and externally. Developing emotional intelligence involves understanding and managing one's emotions effectively. This can help individuals navigate emotional vulnerabilities and make more rational decisions.

Resilience Building: Resilience is the ability to bounce back from adversity. Building resilience involves developing coping strategies, seeking support when needed, and learning from setbacks.

Physical Fitness: Taking care of one's physical health through regular exercise, a balanced diet, meditations, conscious fasts, and adequate rest can mitigate physical vulnerabilities and enhance overall well-being. "For bodily exercise profiteth little: but godliness is profitable unto all things, having promise of the life that is now and that which is to come" 1 Tim 4:8.

Mindfulness and Stress Management: Practicing mindfulness and stress management techniques can help individuals cope with psychological vulnerabilities and reduce the negative impact of stress and anxiety. Have enough rest, show gratitude, be content and anxious of nothing, practice breathing exercises, read the scriptures, eat well, pray and love more and clean your environment are ways of achieving or maintaining a sound mind.

Social Support: Building a strong support network of friends and family can help individuals navigate social vulnerabilities and receive emotional support when facing challenges. All the people in your acquaintance were once strangers so do not be afraid to establish new relationships. It takes conscious efforts to keep a healthy and beneficial relationship. As a family man, a priest, a countryman or a Saint, you do not live unto yourself but unto GOD and your people. Mentorship: Seek out mentors who can provide guidance and wisdom based on their experiences. Our spirit level determines or reflects or state and condition. It takes the Spirit of Christ or individuals at a higher spirit level to raise a person's spirit level.

Adaptation and Innovation: Embracing change and being adaptable in the face of technological disruptions can help individuals thrive in a rapidly evolving world. Accept changes as your survival demands without losing your identity in Christ.

Healthcare and Preventative Measures: To address susceptibility to disease, individuals can prioritize healthcare, self-care, and preventative measures such as physical exercise, regular check-ups, and a healthy lifestyle. Your health as measured by the quality of your vibratory energy and state of mind largely depends on what you eat both physically and spiritually. "But he answered and said, it is written, Man shall not live by bread alone, but by every word that proceedth out of the mouth of God" Mat 4:4. Be careful of what you eat, for not everything that is sold or offered to you as food is good for you. We have one body or perhaps can't afford a double, this house of your spirit can limit your manifestation of God.

Hard Work and Dedication: Success often requires hard work and dedication. Be willing to put in the effort to achieve your goals and mind your business. Hard work towards another's business profits little but hard work for one's own business profits unto higher life, for time and financial freedom. It's never easy to change one's state of rest (location, mentally relaxed state, focus, comfort zone) to do anything. Overcoming the edge, barriers, and horizon unto new frontiers is life's challenge in manifesting our true self, GOD Spirit, and purpose in us. Yet not all these challenges we face are natural. Be able to discern between challenges and threats to your life and goals.

Ethical Behavior: Practicing ethical behavior in one's interactions with others can help build trust and reduce vulnerability to manipulation or exploitation. As Christians our moral and ethical life originates from GOD and the Word of GOD, which is Christ. Upholding personal values and maintaining integrity can provide a strong moral compass and guide decision-making in ethically challenging situations.

Goal Setting and Planning: Setting clear goals and creating plans to achieve them can help individuals focus on their long-term objectives and mitigate the influence of short-term vulnerabilities. Remember quitters always quit with the hope of winning the next or another. By attempting several opportunities, they lose focus, lack consistency and courage to carry on. For winners, they are consistent at one goal or prioritize and persevere in spite of challenges even when failure is in sight just to learn from the experience to never repeat the failure in the next endeavor.

Continuous Improvement: Embracing a mindset of continuous improvement means constantly seeking opportunities for growth and development in all aspects of life. Remember that success is a highly personal and evolving concept. However, success is not solely measured by financial wealth but also by personal growth, fulfillment, and the positive impact you make on the world. You can not give what you don't have. Yet within the spirit of man is all things pertaining to life and godliness. Work on yourself to manifest the manifold treasure and riches hidden in this earthen vessel.

The Council of Living Saints understands that it is ungodly to assume that all non-Christians are devils. At individual levels, a Saint or not, each soul must contribute to their development and overcome life's challenges, old self/lower self. Nevertheless, in Ephesians 6:12 (King James Version) the Bible talks about our wrestle not [just] against flesh and blood, but against principalities, against powers, against the rulers of the darkness of this world, against spiritual wickedness in high places. At the community level, are the Creators of the Systems, the Ombudsman/Watchers, and the Consumers of the systems. The Council of Living Saints as the watchers ensures that the systems of life are life unto life; peaceful, ethical, moral, righteous, and just.

CHAPTER 7

1-Meditation

Deem your constructive connections, networking, relationships, and associations as wealth transactions - CONNECT TRANSACTION. Since information is KEY and everyone knows but not ALL, seek to connect and interact wisely.

2-Meditation

Know that there is Opportunity Cost to the thought you entertain at every instant, the resulting decision you produce, and the actions you pursue/attain. Leave not to chance knowingly or unknowingly, either way is opportunity cost.

3-Meditation

Using AI to create a person or people's future, reality, and interactions with or without their knowledge to your advantage and for control is not fair and just. That's cheating. But who is the judge?

4-Meditation

GOD, from whom all things came has CALLED all things unto himself. This is a journey and a salvation work. Yet few are chosen for the salvation work reconciling all things with GOD unto himself.

5-Meditation

Woe unto a people and a sad place to be for a people to think that there is nothing to do about a toxic leader & cannot associate life as a consequence of the leader's (primary thinker) actions. Such a leader, if not the cause of such vulnerability (gain by inheritance) takes advantage.

6-Meditation

At the fall of the Roman Empire the ruling class/gods amorphized/metamorphosed into a different system/structure of governance where the subjects knew not that they still ruled.

7-Meditation

"JESUS ANSWERED THEM, HAVE NOT I CHOSEN YOU TWELVE, AND ONE OF YOU IS A DEVIL?" JOHN 6:70

8-Meditation

We've seen people that hated each other but found LOVE. Another that loved, married, and yet divorced. Yes, unexplained love can get you married but it takes growth and effort to stay in LOVE/relationship. Equally caring, devoting, forgiving, motivating, not offending...

9-Meditation

People will hear alright, but a mass audience will listen to the speaker who expresses and projects power and authority.

10-Meditation

Be careful not to make a universal (eternal) law based on a singular occurrence or your interpretation of scriptures.

11-Meditation

A Saint once asked, The Elohim (Gods) said "Let Us make mankind in Our image, after Our likeness, ... So, God created man in His own image, in the image and likeness of God He created him; male and female He created them." Which of the Gods' image is the female? Seek, ask & find.

12-Meditation

By the law of Survival, there is abundance of resources able to sustain a man (life) in the land wherever he was born. This is a law and never fails despite the destruction, ignorance, artificial lack, poverty, deprivation, and corruption of and by devils who rule the land.

13-Meditation

No, not eye for eye, for vengeance is the Lord's. Vengeance implies past offense. But in the moment of offense, the law of survival demands actions to resist a devil and stop evil then and in the future. How dreadful it is to fall into the wrath and vengeance of GOD? Save the lost.

14-Meditation

I AM BECAUSE YOU ARE I AM.

15-Meditation

How can any Saint be likened to or called a sheep accepting such an identity? Yes, there are sheep among us, but the Salvation Plan is to make lions out of sheep. A sheep is naturally humble (noun) but a lion that likens itself a sheep is humble (verb). Choice and action make you humble but not the humbled is humble.

16-Meditation

To live in lack is earthly, manly, and hell but abundance is heavenly, Godly, and paradise.

17-Meditation

We have seen but a sad reality that both the intelligent and those who lack the ability of reasoning can be deceived though it's not easy and for long to deceive the former. Yet when deceived they believe with their whole heart "another gospel" thinking that will save them, only becoming condemned, and spiritually deficient the more and more they believe regardless of the rewards, and blessings they think they receive. (Christ will say I know you not). Remember he that is deceived doesn't know he is deceived. How can one believing be condemned by the very things he believes to save? So true is the saying "Believing I am condemned with the unbeliever yet believing I have suffered and endured. What use is my belief?" Oh, wretched man who can save himself from the devils? How do you know that you serve the one true GOD, or you are in a living church? Why are you offended by these things? Maybe you are having a righteous anger unto an awakening. Know that salvation is of the Lord. Yes, the Lord knows your love and heart for him but may be misplaced Just like Saul. In His time but now will turn you into Paul when you see the light, the true light that shatters the veil of lies and falsehood.

18-Meditation

It all collapses if there is no good law and order, enforcement, or blatant disregard with impunity when the rulers partially apply or are above the law. Death manifest where there is no knowledge and application of the law of life just as darkness creeps in where light dimmers.

19-Meditation

"FOR THOUGH THERE BE THAT ARE CALLED GODS, WHETHER IN HEAVEN OR IN EARTH, (AS THERE BE GODS MANY, AND LORDS MANY,); BUT TO US THERE IS BUT ONE GOD, THE FATHER, OF WHOM ARE ALL THINGS, AND WE IN HIM; AND ONE LORD JESUS CHRIST, BY WHOM ARE ALL THINGS, AND WE BY HIM." 1 COR 8:5,6.

20-Meditation

He who has no selfless sacrifice, loyalty to and love for his people/nation lacks understanding of the church or kingdom of Christ. For as below so as above. I pray and hope that your loyalty and love is to a nation/people of life, peace, freedom, and GOD of and for all. For devils can be loyal to their oath and vow to destruction, loving themselves selfishly according to the survival law. Yet through deceit, murder and stealing of life. To mortal man, their kingdom stands but to the God and the Saints, it is only for a while.

21-Meditation

"THE FEAR OF THE LORD IS TO HATE EVIL: PRIDE, AND ARROGANCY, AND THE EVIL WAY, AND THE FROWARD MOUTH, DO I HATE." PROV. 8:13

22-Meditation

How can we expect a man's enemies to tell his truth willingly?

23-Meditation

Words without the power (in the sound) thereof cannot explain Spiritual things but it's canal. Always seek the spirit of a word to understand what the Spirit is saying. "Word Gaslighting" is a tool mightily used by devils to lie, destroy, and make the word of GOD of no effect.

24-Meditation

First, we need to understand that words either sound or written communicate meaning. No word can adequately express a meaning. So, when the prophets wrote whatever the Holy Spirit or angels told them, we lost (say at least 1% of meaning) when they wrote them. And if it was written by a prophet hearing another speak then about 10% meaning was likely lost. From there any translation of the original writings to another language loose meaning because no translation can 100% communicate the original. Also note that those who translated most of the new ones were not native to the language of the prophets who wrote the original scriptures. Also, most of these translators were scholars not necessarily

Hebrews or Christians. More importantly what do you expect from Satan and the devils? If Jesus himself, they killed what prevents them from adulterating his words. Yes, a lot of meaning is missing from some of these new translations. Nevertheless, we count on the Spirit of GOD, the original author to reveal and help our understanding as we read any scripture.

25-Meditation

Who said a mere mortal/human's fight with gods/lords/powers/principals/...for freedom and eternal life would be easy even with the help of GOD? As if man was made/born to be a slave to the authorities.

26-Meditation

Train up a child the way he must go...
No one grows without a training. No training is a kind of training in itself. Growing, a kid must grow. When grown, whatever way he goes is because of a training/rearing/raising by you (parents) or by someone else or by the world. For a way we must or we will all go but not everyone goes THE way of LIFE/GOD.

27-Meditation

When you have done all that you could and know to do, and still not there, know that there is (still) always a way and something else you can do or not do that you don't know yet.

28-Meditation

No matter how hard the circumstances maybe or how hard you might have fell, know that this too shall come to pass, but it shall become past or the past to come to pass again depending on your current actions and response. Be still, have faith, fight on, and never give up on life.

29-Meditation

"BLESSED ARE THE PEACEMAKERS: FOR THEY SHALL BE CALLED THE CHILDREN OF GOD." MATT. 5:9.

How did You miss your blessings? For you have failed to arbitrate and seek peace? You knew the supposed invasion in advance, warned but did not intervene peacefully by virtue of dialogue, mediation, and diplomacy. And you know the 'friend' can't win yet you encourage and enable them to fight on to their doom and the suffering of the world. Seek peace and life.

30-Meditation

With the mental health crisis and spiritual deficiency rampant in the world, our commission and ministries are more urgent and needful now. For darkness is over the surface of the earth. Let us shine the light more than ever. You are light. Shine, Love, faith and hope toward the world.

31-Meditation

Faithful in the physical sense is loyalty, truthfulness, consistency, or stewardship. This is very important to one's survival. In the system of the world, this is a requirement for a subordinate going about another man's business while requiring a faithful adherence by the owner to this mutual agreement. Let not the wicked take advantage of your faithfulness. Be faithful about another's as unto your own business.

In the spiritual sense, the faithful don't live by sight but by faith. Live by sight/faith is inferred by your responses, both internal and external reactions, decisions, speech and dispositions to circumstances and events according to the sensory organs/regenerated spirit.

The faithful applies faith looking into the future. He acknowledges GOD in all his ways. Faithfulness is his lifestyle and believe system.

He is faithful he that has grown and unified his instincts into trust in power of GOD. His reasoning is renewed & judgement is faith (religion) based.

He is faithful of Christ, he that believes in the resurrection and resurrection power of Christ.

He is faithful, he that sees hope in all dead situations.

He is faithful, he that endures persecution for (his beliefs), His names sake.

He is faithful, he that stands for the right reasons when he knows doing so can cost him his life.

He is faithful, he that obeys/lives the commandments of Christ.

He is faithful he that loves with the love of GOD not the love of man (love based on survival).

He is faithful, he that walks in the spirit not in the flesh.

He is faithful, he that loves and lives in righteousness.

He is faithful he that works his faith to apply the power of GOD within him and make all things possible.

He is faithful, he that is Godly.

He is faithful he that....

32-Meditation

Lack is oppressive, so is poverty depressing. Hope that you're not crushed, have faith to overcome, patient to endure, share & love to rejoice in what you have. Greed & selfishness; sins, laziness GOD hate. Be mindful of artificial & carnal desires that drain minds and drown souls.

33-Meditation

Blessed (enjoying enviable happiness, spiritually prosperous—with life-joy and satisfaction in God's favor and salvation, regardless of their outward conditions) are the makers and maintainers of peace, for they shall be called the sons of God! But for the sons of devil, we know your works. Treacherous, makers of war, orchestrator of divisions, contentions, and chaos. Breakers of the divine law: LAW OF LIFE. Infiltrators and Invaders (visible or not) of the Church.
"HE THAT COMMITTETH SIN IS OF THE DEVIL; FOR THE DEVIL SINNETH FROM THE BEGINNING. FOR THIS PURPOSE THE SON OF GOD WAS MANIFESTED, THAT HE MIGHT DESTROY THE WORKS OF THE DEVIL." 1 JOH 3:8.

34-Meditation

Understanding or one's perception is not attained in a vacuum. So, the desired understanding of a material requires a BASIS to be meaningful or else you get a random meaning or misunderstanding which in itself is understanding but not as intended by the author. A BASIS is therefore the prerequisite and the building block for understanding.

35-Meditation

Nobody needs to be watched more than the leader. Watch not only to follow rightly but monitor and hold accountable.

36-Meditation

"IF ANY MAN SEE HIS BROTHER SIN A SIN WHICH IS NOT UNTO DEATH, HE SHALL ASK, AND HE SHALL GIVE HIM LIFE FOR THEM THAT SIN NOT UNTO DEATH. THERE IS A SIN UNTO DEATH: I DO NOT SAY THAT HE SHALL PRAY FOR IT. ALL UNRIGHTEOUSNESS IS SIN: AND THERE IS A SIN NOT UNTO DEATH." 1 JOHN 5:16-17

37-Meditation

Do not hastily correct a fool, for a fool is wise in his own eyes. The wise is a fool in another's eyes. It's wisdom in itself to acknowledge one's ignorance and obtain a teachable spirit.

38-Meditation

Love is not the forgiveness of the guilty in denial of justice to the victim and order but rather the exercise of mercy in Judgment. GOD is Just. In HIS grace we found mercy, from which we receive forgiveness.

39-Meditation

I love GOD so I love life. You are life and precious more than any eye or mind can perceive. Live for life not death.

40-Meditation

The human mind is capable of believing in anything or nothing. A man can be made to believe anything or nothing. Anything or nothing is a man's truth. That's a man has lied or believed in a lie at some time. Tragically some may believe in a lie all the time or all their lives. GOD save us.

41-Meditation

Yes, it's good to give to the poor but for what good when you continue to approve of measures or turn a blind eye to the cause, if not the cause of poverty yourself. It is a greater good to resist the evil that turns people poor in mind, in spirit and in estate.

42-Meditation

The first level of reasoning is to ask questions, comprehension challenges the answer while finding wisdom in the next question to ask.

43-Meditation

A move TO or IN ones' advantage is Favor.

44-Meditation

A flash of consciousness in time and space.

45-Meditation

There is a Neurogen that is excreted at the trigger of luxury and comfortable experience and another by misery and suffering that shapes one's mode and personality.

46-Meditation

There appears to be an agenda that humans will not reproduce normally but that by a controlled birthing system of just the selected few and a factory of mass production, SPECIFICITY and MIXING are possibilities. In the end just order or shop an offspring. Fate of humanity.

47-Meditation

Are mind parasites real? Soul eaters.

48-Meditation

The future: next moment, minute, hours, days is like a clean canvas that is and must be painted by you or someone else present or past. It comes into the now never blank, like it or not, it becomes the reality. Can you erase the canvas?

49-Meditation

It's the DUTY to LIFE to fight or resist evil WITHIN and WITHOUT as long as you live in this world.

Oh Saint "...put on the new man, which after God is created in righteousness and true holiness" And when you have overcome the EVIL WITHIN know that evil still exist, for not all men even know of the evil within, while some accept its power over them and oppose it not. Fight!

50-Meditation

Spiritual INSTRUCTIONS from GOD like Policies need directives and procedures (mantras) to override and overwrite every opposing pre-existing stronghold, paradigms, predispositions and earthly standards in order to practically or materially do the WORD not just obey continually.

51-Meditation

For the fear of death, who delivers man at all ages from medical and pharmaceutical slavery and tyranny. Those they trust! "And except those days should be shortened, there should no flesh be saved: but for the elect's sake those days shall be shortened" For flesh on earth will be changed in those days.

52-Meditation

A toxic leader or governance is a fearful tragedy, deception and dangerous when a puppet. For their damage is beyond the third and fourth generation. May create systems for perpetual reign unknown to the subject victims. Liberation is by External Redeemers or Internal Awakeners.

53-Meditation

The rise of the Sons of Anak, the creatures "BUT AS THE DAYS OF NOE WERE, SO SHALL ALSO THE COMING OF THE SON OF MAN BE." MATT. 24:37.

"THAT THE SONS OF GOD SAW THE DAUGHTERS OF MEN THAT THEY WERE FAIR; AND THEY TOOK THEM WIVES OF ALL WHICH THEY CHOSE. AND THE LORD SAID, MY SPIRIT SHALL NOT ALWAYS STRIVE WITH MAN, FOR THAT HE ALSO IS FLESH: YET HIS DAYS SHALL BE AN HUNDRED AND TWENTY YEARS. THERE WERE GIANTS IN THE EARTH IN THOSE DAYS; AND ALSO AFTER THAT, WHEN THE SONS OF GOD CAME IN UNTO THE DAUGHTERS OF MEN, AND THEY BARE CHILDREN TO THEM, THE SAME BECAME MIGHTY MEN WHICH WERE OF OLD, MEN OF RENOWN. AND GOD SAW THAT THE

WICKEDNESS OF MAN WAS GREAT IN THE EARTH, AND THAT EVERY IMAGINATION OF THE THOUGHTS OF HIS HEART WAS ONLY EVIL CONTINUALLY. AND IT REPENTED THE LORD THAT HE HAD MADE MAN ON THE EARTH, AND IT GRIEVED HIM AT HIS HEART." GENESIS 6:2-6.

We know your works and they are evil upon earth. Yet the Lord with the Saints descends upon you with swift judgement and justice that you will cease to exist in the land of the living. Redemption for any? LORD only knows. "FOR THE EARNEST EXPECTATION OF THE CREATURE WAITETH FOR THE MANIFESTATION OF THE SONS OF GOD." ROMANS 8:19. *How did they become giants but in the minds?*

54-Meditation

Every matter decay and diffuses. Be equally concerned about mundane and futile stuff, gases (kept) around you (live in) that you inhale or absorb and cloud your mind as smoke.

55-Meditation

Emotions are powerful human experience, expression, and assets that if one doesn't intelligently control can be destructive or weaponized against the individual.

56-Meditation

The righteous judge knows that the evil man is himself a victim of a greater evil. It's a greater evil for a devil to make evil out of a man.

57-Meditation

A system in operation is as good as the people running it. A (racist) system that targets a group may not necessarily be against specific individuals of the group. When there is nothing you know you can do as an individual don't play a victim yet don't forget your group identity.

58-Meditation

It is a greater good that the stronger/more powerful/richer in this life among you act GOODLY (just, serve, defend, and sacrifice) by the weak, poor and the have-nots. Terrible and Terrific the world would be if no one cares about the other?

59-Meditation

"FINALLY, BRETHREN, WHATSOEVER THINGS ARE TRUE, WHATSOEVER THINGS ARE HONEST, WHATSOEVER THINGS ARE JUST, WHATSOEVER THINGS ARE PURE, WHATSOEVER THINGS ARE LOVELY, WHATSOEVER THINGS ARE OF GOOD REPORT; IF THERE BE ANY VIRTUE, AND IF THERE BE ANY PRAISE, THINK ON THESE THINGS." PHILIPPIANS 4:8

60-Meditation

You reap WHAT you SOW. If your actions are seeds you sow, then the thoughts behind them are the mother of the seeds. For sowing as you live you must sow but sadly others may plant them unbeknownst to you. Yet you reap whatever sown magnified or not in your subconsciousness or spirit.

61-Meditation

The RIGHTEOUS shall LIVE by FAITH, not by SIGHT. LIVE, not just physically (SIGHT) but eternally and spiritually (FAITH) in CHRIST.

62-Meditation

What must be done has to be done. No excuse, tarry not, stay focused, don't give up, may not always be easy, comfortable, or familiar yet just get it done. Do the right thing and be at peace with yourself.

63-Meditation

Yes, there are barriers, disadvantages, unfairness, racism, lack, devils, and demons. Yet you can beat the odds if you can have a higher Subject-Mental-State (SMS). It's truth that the world will pay high (salary) for an acquired, advanced trained SMS. Don't forget FAITH although fundamental is SMS. If not, why the need for spiritual teachers and the Holy Spirit as a teacher or the School of the Apostles or the Prophets? We ask a child 'What will you become when you grow up?'. It's the same as what will your SMS be. For the sake of survival law (comfortable standard of living) and law of life please become SOMEBODY and if you become somebody, be SOMEONE Righteous, Just, and Love. Have faith, and also, have SMS. Train your mind.

64-Meditation

It's foolishness to pray for long life without health, wealth, faith and meaningful worth. GOD gives all, why ask for one without these? Unless you seek life from Him that has but not all. The blessing of the LORD makes a person rich, and he adds no sorrow to it. Seek all lest you curse GOD at your PRIME, or by your ungloried life and at old age if still have awareness plead for death out of misery and loneliness. For I know the plans I have for you," saith the LORD, "FOR I KNOW THE THOUGHTS THAT I THINK TOWARD YOU, SAITH THE LORD, THOUGHTS OF PEACE, AND NOT OF EVIL, TO GIVE YOU AN EXPECTED END." JEREMIAH 29:11

65-Meditation

You are not a devil because we don't believe the same thing but because you steal, destroy, and kill life even one of your own. That is evil.

66-Meditation

The history books available to the public are just a created narrative from the BEGINNING but not beyond. Well, any moment in time and space in the expanse is a beginning.

67-Meditation

Your reality can be your awareness and disposition. Input is data/knowledge or predispositions, then processing and derivatives of information, and the resulting/output disposition and perception creates your locked in or cyclical reality.

68-Meditation

Do not respond in doubt, talk lack or give in to fear when the world, universe, or situations require of you or there exist a need to expend a resource or draw from within. For you are not required of what you don't already have.

The Council Of Living Saints
The Meditations Of A Christian Saint

69-Meditation

Either physical or mental trials, as depicted in the Bible, Jesus prevailed by countering Satan with scriptures. Similarly, we find victory against any thoughts, imaginations, or paradigms opposing our faith, abilities, and life with the divine words of GOD."

70-Meditation

There was no life but chaos until there was law and order. So, GOD said let there be...

71-Meditation

You are responsible for your life any time you speak or impress upon your subconsciousness the words;
I AM ...
I HAVE...
I WILL...
No matter what, let whatever follows I... be positive for it's your command and creativity to the universal intelligence, spirits, and matter.

72-Meditation

No word you ever spoke or thought you ever imagined goes away without manifestation in one form or the other.

73-Meditation

Christendom was never meant to be an NGO or some nonprofit organization but rather a nation, country, and kingdom yet without an earthly king or small group of leadership and subjects.

74-Meditation

How do you save a people from their slave master that they know not but love dearly? You are likely going to be their enemy. Remember the same voice that exalted hosanna screamed crucify him crucify him.

75-Meditation

In a day there are thousands of ethers of thoughts originating from our senses with the world or active in our subconsciousness. We all dream, imagine or desire but he that match his attitude with his desire, focus his WILL while confessing the fulfillment has whatever he willed.

76-Meditation

There is a sense or assurance of confidence, intellect, sanity, realism when finally, one finds another that is likeminded or affirms one's truth, reality or thought. However, that doesn't mean that such conviction or reality is TRUE. For falsehood also has believers.

77-Meditation

Jesus died for everyone. That every man and all by the crucifixion destroy lower self for the new man created in the likeness of GOD, the greater I AM within, the holy and righteousness to live in this flesh and life.

The Council Of Living Saints
The Meditations Of A Christian Saint

78-Meditation

The LORD thy God is one. No matter how ugly or beautiful you may think you are, GOD is like you outwardly/internally. He who sees God in an image other than himself worships another God.

79-Meditation

To reject spiritual speaking in tongues is likened to rejecting the fact that babies and toddlers or you once spoke in tongues. There is in fact the language of the gods or spirits.

80-Meditation

CAUTION, know that not everything sold at the store or labeled food or offered to you as food is safe or is GOOD for you. You need a healthy and lively body to fully function on earth.

81-Meditation

It is mass deception to think or believe that there are only two main religions by the numbers. Or there exist only the religions you know. What happened to the enemies of GOD in the bible? Did they perish with their religion at the advent of Christ? What religion then rules the world?

82-Meditation

The robots have always been walking among man long before you know.

83-Meditation

Can the balls be chipped? Who seeks to know? All things imagined are possible?

84-Meditation

As kids we were carried to and from and decided for not only because we were weak in strength and minds but because the adults understand had responsibilities to raising us. What if even as adults ourselves there are stronger and more intelligent grownups, visible or invincible humans or not-so-humans that still considers us as kids regardless of our age. Woe unto you that refuses to grow up after knowing the need to. Remember, not all kids are treated with love, kindness, care or equally by these grownups. Be whole in Spirit, Body, and Mind.

85-Meditation

What you know you are is a fraction of who you really are. What you know if you knew is what you remember at any instant but not all you know that you can recollect on demand. If only you can remember, you are more than you know.

86-Meditation

He who wants to understand what IS must also seek out what IS is not.

The Council Of Living Saints
The Meditations Of A Christian Saint

87-Meditation

How can you reap that of, from and out of man that which is not planted in him? Except for the rare occasions of self-cultivation. Sow or nurture that which you seek out of a man. This is a rule of the gods. Listen, you that hears.

88-Meditation

Mind your expectations of another. You may never know what in the heart has been planted by another. "KEEP AND GUARD YOUR HEART WITH ALL VIGILANCE AND ABOVE ALL THAT YOU GUARD, FOR OUT OF IT FLOW THE SPRINGS OF LIFE". PROVERBS 4:23

89-Meditation

In today's world and structure of governance, truth and reality is the law the leaders make or verdict the judge or court rule and the propaganda the media relay.

90-Meditation

You are not awake yet nor are you regenerated if you've not discovered all the lies you have believed since childhood. The World is a big lie. ...yea, "THEY SHALL PUT YOU OUT OF THE SYNAGOGUES: YEA, THE TIME COMETH, THAT WHOSOEVER KILLETH YOU WILL THINK THAT HE DOETH GOD SERVICE." JOHN 16:2.

Examine yourself. GOD help us.

91-Meditation

There are both artificial and innate, physical, and immaterial barriers to total freedom, self-awareness, and actualization. The vail of Satan, LACK, the circumference of reality, limiting boundaries of consciousness/spirit. How the infinite and formless spirit and mind is capsulated in mortal and confined flesh, shapes and forms on earth, or others worlds is a wonder if not a miracle. These boundaries although not all created by man, the devils have ensured their perpetual existence. To break free takes GRACE, knowledge, courage, faith, and love.

92-Meditation

I hope sooner than later you realize that you are more than you think and know you are. Most of us know ourselves in the light of definitions and labels engraved upon us by parents, neighborhood, and system of the world like religion, education, and the government. You are not just your name, degree, job, house, car, or a mistake. You are more than these. You know it very well and that's why sometimes you get frustrated, sad, and angry. I hope soon the real you will be revealed. The great, powerful, awesome, and mighty you. Keep trying, keep searching, keep hoping, keep praying, keep working, keep fighting and never give up. Some things in this world you will have to do for yourself. This message may be all the help you need from another at this time.

93-Meditation

For how long should we continue to watch this world staged movie? They that know cannot wait but know the Best Is Yet To Come.

94-Meditation

The system of the world and man state of mind is such that the world could be easily, if not already colonized by some more intelligent beings or another man with power of AI clothed in a silicon body or body double. Don't people select more intelligent people to rule over them?

95-Meditation

If all that we know was from outside of ourselves, we would be the most miserable creatures. The makers, gods and devils will enslave and program us forever at their will. Thank GOD and never underestimate the power of the Holy Spirit, inspirations, reasoning, revelation, visions, and meditation.

96-Meditation

Your life experience is a continuous spectrum of awareness/consciousness that can be quantified as information assimilated creating your reality. Reality is defined by your perception, believes, opinions and spiritual orientation. Falsehood, deception, and illusions are the weapons of devils without which evil cannot prevail (over man) are at times the same tool to save the people from the devils. Salvation plan is always a mystery, the enemy sees it unfold yet understand it not, miscalculate or is deceived.
"WHICH NONE OF THE PRINCES OF THIS WORLD KNEW: FOR HAD THEY KNOWN IT, THEY WOULD NOT HAVE CRUCIFIED THE LORD OF GLORY." 1 COR. 2:8.

97-Meditation

We all make mistakes. Some mistakes are silly, irritating, uneducated, dangerous, fatal, tragic, sin or harmless, innocent, naive, insightful, opportunity, a lesson if learnt is a step towards excellence or perfection. Any path taken shall end you somewhere. Grow up, life to life.

98-Meditation

The Gospel according to our eternal revelations must not to be bent, modified, sweetened, or blended for anyone. The Gospel is for both the living and the dead but not all life forms or humans will receive. Your revelation is not for everyone. Them that you're sent to will receive you.

99-Meditation

"I BESEECH YOU THEREFORE, BRETHREN, BY THE MERCIES OF GOD, THAT YE PRESENT YOUR BODIES A LIVING SACRIFICE, HOLY, ACCEPTABLE UNTO GOD, WHICH IS YOUR REASONABLE SERVICE." ROM. 12:1.

100-Meditation

For life's sake do something Good, free yourself from mental slavery and survival plane, seek for better self, free from penury, self-doubt, guilt, hate, despair, condemnation, overly contentment. Don't be selfish. These do, if not for yourself at least for humanity, life unto life.

101-Meditation

Jesus the Christ is the only man known to have challenged and made public spectacle of the gods and faced the almost inevitable, shameful, agonizing death of a Cross. These have ruled man for ages to the destruction of man. Who can save if not this same Jesus Christ and the Way.

102-Meditation

We, all are from the same source of life (GOD), formless, infinite spirit with consciousness seeking to manifest in a mundane, mortal, limiting world. Someday I pray you may find the joy and happiness in fully expressing and sharing yourself for life unto life here on earth.

103-Meditation

The Old Testament, dispensation and disposition taught man to Obey and work today to become tomorrow. The new age teaches to Be or Act today what you are or want to Become tomorrow. This is the Law of Faith. This is not just for Christians. The challenge is to become, believing, acting like what you are but not yet seen. You can't become who are not. Who are you? What do you know about You? Are you all that you see, what others say about you? Who do you think or know you are? Not all are true. Today, you can choose to know what GOD says you are. And what does GOD say you are? This is truth you are not all that we See you are. Stop believing the lesser of you: weak, stupid, ugly, liar ... This is a call to the one greater in you. The great, marvelous, and beautiful one born after GOD. That's who GOD says you are. Like the mango tree cannot bear orange fruit [unless GMO], so you can't be what you are not. You can't pray to be righteous, rich, or work, or hope to be. You pray or work at it because you were created rich and righteous. You are not your body. You are of GOD. Whenever you say I AM ... Say who you are, not who you are by what you see outwardly or feel. That's the challenge. How hard it's for you to say, act and be I Am not a sinner? So, it is hard to say, be or act I Am not poor.

Be free, look into the mirror of life and truth and forget not who you truly are. Don't conform to worldly and slavery thinking. You are great, special gift from GOD, a blessing to the Church and a miracle for the world.

104-Meditation

Do you say what you mean or mean what you say? Maybe you can be more truthful or be well understood if you understand these things.

105-Meditation

A word represents meaning. Meaning is distinct but the word to describe it is insufficient, limited and varies due to language. Understand that no word in itself is sufficient to describe intended meaning. Not all languages come close to meaning. Meaning is universal but the words are not.

106-Meditation

We have seen an evil far greater than demons and that's the power of ignorance. Seek knowledge, search for truth and in all your getting, gain Wisdom. Wisdom is life.

107-Meditation

There is still hope when it seems all is over. God is not done yet in fact is never done making things better. Look up to the Lord, trust him and believe in his WORD. He is working all things for your good. Yes you, for you and for your GOOD.

108-Meditation

The times where violent wars were used to depopulate humanity seems to be over. Now the devils have 1001 ways to depopulate whilst people unknowingly cheer their own destruction. Biological weapons? War on humanity.

109-Meditation

Meeting the physical needs of the people through miracles, compassion, and kindness was no doubt the reason for Jesus's successful ministry. So, since you know you can't perform such/any miracle yet what must you do as a minister? Jesus healed, maybe have a hospital; he fed 5000, have a food bank; he blessed little children have scholarships and education centers; he cast out demons have prayer camps and rehabs; he ..., have ...!!! There is more you can do for your ministry. Faith without works is dead.

110-Meditation

I is poor but I Am is rich,
I is ignorant and silly, but I Am knows and is wise,
I is lack but I Am is abundant,
I is temporal but I Am is eternal,
I is earthly but I Am is heavenly,
I is carnal but I Am is divine,
For I to become who I Am is the ultimate purpose of life.

111-Meditation

What does it mean to speak evil of another? "TO SPEAK EVIL OF NO MAN, TO BE NO BRAWLERS, BUT GENTLE, SHEWING ALL MEEKNESS UNTO ALL MEN." TIT 3:2. This is normally explained as gossiping. But not so. Compare the two translations
KJV: To speak evil of no man, to be no brawlers, but gentle,

shewing all meekness unto all men.

AMP: To slander or abuse or speak evil of no one, to avoid being contentious, to be forbearing (yielding, gentle, and conciliatory), and to show unqualified courtesy toward everybody. It is important to know that we should not;
1. Slander
2. Falsely accuse
3. Cause strife and contention
4. Take pleasure in another's Misfortune
5. Despise
6. Judgmentally condemn
7. Divinate, enchant, bewitch, conjure, cast spell, or pray evil for another.

However, we should never fail to know the truth. For instance, our conversation that seek the truth or talk about the evil work of another whoever maybe is not speaking evil of another. Telling, exposing, or listening to the truth of a Church member or Pastor's corruption, hypocrisy, or evil ways is not speaking evil. Nothing is hidden that will not be brought to light.

Note the difference between

1. Speaking evil of another

2. Speaking of the evil of another.

So don't think you can hide your evil ways under this verse and falsely preach Titus 3:2. Remember when John the Baptist spoke about the evil Of King Herod.

Remember what Jesus Christ spoke of the Pharisees. It is our duty as Saints to expose evil but not in a manner of declaring external condemnation of another. "FOR WE OURSELVES ALSO

WERE SOMETIMES FOOLISH, DISOBEDIENT, DECEIVED, SERVING DIVERS LUSTS AND PLEASURES, LIVING IN MALICE AND ENVY, HATEFUL, AND HATING ONE ANOTHER. BUT AFTER THAT THE KINDNESS AND LOVE OF GOD OUR SAVIOUR TOWARD MAN APPEARED, NOT BY WORKS OF RIGHTEOUSNESS WHICH WE HAVE DONE, BUT ACCORDING TO HIS MERCY HE SAVED US, BY THE WASHING OF REGENERATION, AND RENEWING OF THE HOLY GHOST; WHICH HE SHED ON US ABUNDANTLY THROUGH JESUS CHRIST OUR SAVIOUR;" TITUS 3:3-6

112-Meditation

Where is peace when war can be started and sustained by a lie. Where is freedom of expression and diversity of ideas when censored and forced to keep thoughts to oneself. Without which we are doomed to follow the individual censoring ideals without challenge. Why do you think GOD of love will punish or chastise you more than rewarding you for your good deeds? No deed is without a reward, but GOD is merciful and kind in judgment.

113-Meditation

We are not against a change or new order for justice, equality, love, joy, peace, and righteousness. Of course, when Christ is come there will be a new order. Humanity and creation can't accept or survive any new form of tyranny, oppression, evil and death as a new world order.

114-Meditation

Only a lie must be hidden from scrutiny and criticism to abide for fear of exposure and consequently losing its power of deception.

115-Meditation

"If Elohim said let us make man in our image, male and female created HE them, then which one of the Elohim's images is the female." Good question my child, I said as the Council stood in wonder but not aback at the question.

116-Meditation

Any time you realize that you are alive is the time you start anew. You are alive start living.

117-Meditation

It is better not to bathe than to bathe with contaminated water. Let your waters be clean.

118-Meditation

A man's mind can be limited by the limiting space or vastness of his environment or imagination.

119-Meditation

Unfamiliarity engenders uncertainty but not fear, else you will never try. It's new not a nay. Ask Wisdom and don't hesitate to apply the power, the grace of GOD and wisdom within you.

120-Meditation

Stupidity can be very costly. Since no system available and accessible to an individual or group can completely dissolve it, one must be in perpetual education of oneself. Be wise and humble, it's just a matter of time, place, condition and/or a wiser one to prove you stupid.

121-Meditation

The one who only lives by, in, with and off a lie is amoral, refuse and oppose the truth even unto others. But the one who is made to live a lie or deceived is demoralized and cannot discern TRUTH.

122-Meditation

"FOR THE FATHER JUDGETH NO MAN, BUT HATH COMMITTED ALL JUDGMENT UNTO THE SON:" JOH. 5:22

123-Meditation

"DO YE NOT KNOW THAT THE SAINTS SHALL JUDGE THE WORLD? AND IF THE WORLD SHALL BE JUDGED BY YOU, ARE YE UNWORTHY TO JUDGE THE SMALLEST MATTERS? KNOW YE NOT THAT WE SHALL JUDGE ANGELS? HOW MUCH MORE THINGS THAT PERTAIN TO THIS LIFE?" 1 COR. 6:2-3

124-Meditation

The Church was never meant to exist as a non-profit entity within any nation. In a world where profit and monetary resources wield profound influence over institutions, power dynamics, and access to essential resources, this traditional structure within the contemporary governance systems often leaves the Church, Mount Zion, in a state of financial fragility and ineffectiveness, resulting in its struggle against impoverishment and a sense of defeat.

The ministry of Jesus while on earth was profoundly rich and wealthy ministry. It was a ministry of giving, healing, preaching, reconciliation, and no way surviving on donations (although people donated freely in appreciation not in kind, compulsion or for a need). We are talking of him that found the ends of life; resources or demands, by fishing money [gold], the means in a fish. He is Jesus Christ alive, the head of the Church, the same yesterday, today and forevermore.

125-Meditation

True and righteousness judgment is only by the righteous and christened. Who is he that convict another to death or condemns to hell? As sound as the Law may be, such a ruling by a carnal and unrighteous judge is nothing but murder and a miscarriage of justice yet acceptable in the world.

126-Meditation

Fear GOD, not man as unto yourself or anything that is created. "AND FEAR NOT THEM WHICH KILL THE BODY, BUT ARE NOT ABLE TO KILL THE SOUL: BUT RATHER FEAR HIM WHICH IS ABLE TO DESTROY BOTH SOUL AND BODY IN HELL." MAT. 10:28

Do always not the will of man but the right thing. Turn to life, be bold, and fight on.

127-Meditation

Don't think highly of yourself as you ought to. This is true when talking about wisdom and arrogance. Don't

The Council Of Living Saints
The Meditations Of A Christian Saint

confuse this with you thinking highly of who you are. You are born of GOD.

You are as he is; he is I am that I am.

You are beautiful you are great,

You are a priest of GOD. You are...

As a man thinketh so is he.

Don't accept anything low, or just anything life will throw at you. This life is a great confession. Not what people will say about you or think about you although it's important when the people are your loved ones. It is what you say and think about yourself that matters. Read and listen to Jesus Christ's confession about himself:
I am the light of the world,
I come from above,
Before Abraham was, I am,
I am the way truth...,
I am wiser than Solomon,
I am the resurrection and life,
I and the father are one,
Come to me all Yee heavily ladened.
I am the vine,
I am ...,
What do you say you are? Never think of yourself lowly. It doesn't matter where or what you are now.

You can't be someone that you believe or confess not,

because out of the abundance of heart (spirit) you speak. Have faith in the You, the Spirit of GOD that you are.

For greater is he that you are within than the you, you are without.

128-Meditation

This New Year, The Year of Possibilities.

Fear Not,

Be Free,

Enjoy Life,

Give Life,

Love Life,

For GOD is Love and Life.

129-Meditation

We are all wise in our own eyes but the one who humbly acknowledges;
- his folly and seek to learn from everything and everyone,
-that wisdom is infinite
-that no one has it all is the wiser.

130-Meditation

In times past countries were violently forced into submission and colonization. In our times deception, infiltration, planned sleeper cells, bribery, and coercion. Years in the making, the enemy within when all institutions and democratic apparatus are run by puppets.

The Council Of Living Saints
The Meditations Of A Christian Saint

131-Meditation

Unbeknownst to most people if not all, as if by coincidence the enemy by social, ideological, cultural, and racial divisions, information and psychological operations, institutional decay, economic suicides, and resource theft, a country is destroyed from within and by/with the people.

132-Meditation

Why does Heaven have military and warrior angels? Who do they war against? Woe unto the earth for the Devil cast unto it.

133-Meditation

We have looked and seen that people all over the world love peace, joy, life, and liberty for all but when devils rule, they trample upon the sovereignty, life, and liberty of others from other countries in the name of love for their country.

134-Meditation

How disturbing and troubling it is for devils when a day goes by without any trouble in the land?

135-Meditation

Love your nation. A man's love for his country and quest to live (survive) should not overcome love for life or become enmity to humanity. Humanity is love and respect for life, faith, hope, peace, righteousness, and joy. Let not your quest for your life overcome your humanity.

136-Meditation

What do you do when one's love for his nation becomes an enemy of another? Let no one seek to destroy another from another country. We all belong to the nation of life. Let the latter defend but in love, justice, and peace not tit for tat. Not in vengeance but in respect for life.

137-Meditation

Righteousness and Godliness require you to live the walk of physical life and the walk of spiritual life. You have a duty towards both lives. Ignore none although one is above the other.

138-Meditation

Every idea that was ever imagined...

Every thought that was ever formed

Every word that was ever spoken

Is never lost.

139-Meditation

We're not against unification. We welcome a global effort to unify humanity and all lives as required by survival law without losing our individuality & power of diversity under the law of LIFE. What we warn against is the pretense of globalization by the very few to consolidate power & control.

The Council Of Living Saints
The Meditations Of A Christian Saint

140-Meditation

People associate one's credibility with his personality, relationship, prestige, and titles. Devils destroy a person's credibility with his audience by caricaturizing or lampooning him in the presence of his audience. Wondering why your truth can't still be heard or believed?

141-Meditation

There is a storm upon us. Few are aware, many are impacted. In prayers for Saints and patriots on its wings. Carry on carry on. Do well for justice, truth, peace, life, and liberty. GOD keep you. Save the land. GODWINS!!!

142-Meditation

You are in the world but not of the world. Why then do you believe a Word or spirit or people of the world outside Christ without questioning or reasoning by the Spirit of GOD? Test all spirits.

143-Meditation

We have all asked ourselves once, Are we alone? For us to accept the negative, unchallenged contrary to our inner uncertainty or remain ignorant is deception by design.

144-Meditation

In Times like this when most entertainment is indoctrination and propaganda, it's very damaging to him that seeks to be entertained in every supposed free time or mind. Be more studious, prayerful, meditative, and motivated. Rejoice always but seek to add value to self in all thy ways.

145-Meditation

You can't find your Bible is not an excuse to miss out on evangelism because thinking about the disciples and apostles, they didn't have a Bible. They were the Bible.

146-Meditation

Can one live a day without first dreaming it?

147-Meditation

Worry about nothing. Think about nothing and you'll become nothing. You'll become the object of your focused thinking. Do not worry should not be construed as an absence of thinking. It is the focus of thought on negativity, fear, and despair that rob us of (opportunity cost) peace of mind, joy of the spirit, and critical thin. Examine yourself always.

148-Meditation

It's always time to share and lend some love and care. Doing unto others as you would want to be done unto you. It is strength and power derived from encouraging others in your adversity.

149-Meditation

"Let love be without dissimulation. Abhor that which is evil; cleave to that which is good." Rom 12:9

The Council Of Living Saints
The Meditations Of A Christian Saint

150-Meditation

It is also evil to self and to your people to fail, neglect, and procrastinate the good you know or have to do to survive knowingly and willfully.

151-Meditation

Let your desires so exhume you to consume you unto action and cause. Be exhumed out of the graves of ignorance, procrastination, negligence, irresponsibility, and immaturity. Let not your desire consume you unto evil.

152-Meditation

He is God-like among men who can walk in steps of tomorrow according to the tactically planned orderings of today.

153-Meditation

Angelic Military in heaven? Waaooo what in heaven would God need a military for? Think, the enemy is real. Heaven is worth protecting.

154-Meditation

You did it again Saints, saving humanity. If only the people knew your deeds, you will be hailed as gods. GOD bless you and your service.

155-Meditation

Imagine your flight lands on an unknown island where you all must work together to survive. All 100s of you elect a few to create a system to manage the abundance of resources for all and ensure civility and ensure sustainability. Over time they massed much power and influence to make laws and systems that ensured their survival at the expense of the others and their perpetual rule. They kept knowledge of the outsider world from the people. They worked with but hid the knowledge of the natives on the other side of the island. How can that be possible? Could this be real?

156-Meditation

Think about when you are born into this world. The more you think in parallel. As long as you think your survival is only by self, independent of the community as a whole, we lose, and you definitely lose the most. Life unto life none above or below life. GOD is life.

157-Meditation

Thank you for your service. Yes, regardless of your compensation understand that a good work, job, or position offers you a chance to help others (humanity). Let honesty, integrity, and love lead you for your reward now or in the future is not far from you nor is it only from man.

158-Meditation

Suggestive Thinking is the process of influencing another by subliminal suggestions, sowing thoughts, affirming a thought, supporting recommending, concurring, or validating a thought or act. Can get others to do what they would have never thought of, or are afraid of, or disapprove of.

The Council Of Living Saints
The Meditations Of A Christian Saint

159-Meditation

The first law of life is survival so a man should never be rid of his ability to provide, defend, and protect his life or loved ones. Self-defense against tyranny, oppression, and deception which opposes GOD's will for man is one's solemn duty that can only be shared not delegated or entrusted.

160-Meditation

"Who created heaven and the earth? Genesis God - Chapter 1, Lord God - Chapter 2. What is the difference?" Good question my son. You shall know the truth who that seek.

161-Meditation

Our greatest work is you knowing that in the earth of abundance your seemingly lack, suffering & hardships are not all your fault nor the will (destiny) of GOD but the results of evil and selfishness of the few.

"WHEN THE RIGHTEOUS ARE IN AUTHORITY, THE PEOPLE REJOICE: BUT WHEN THE WICKED BEARETH RULE, THE PEOPLE MOURN." PROVERBS 29:2

162-Meditation

You are a wonderful consciousness like a drop in the ocean of the cosmopolitan. Whether you live on or not in the hereafter, what matters is now. You are alive in an overly abundant and sustainable earth for all. It's the selfishness of the very few devils that all seems impossible, suffering...

163-Meditation

We are all created equal by one spirit of life. Refuse lack, resist the oppressors who see you only as useful means and resources for their existence. Deep within you, you know there is a higher life and experience to attain. Yes, this is possible here and now.

164-Meditation

Seek, explore, and enjoy a life of abundance. This is the will of GOD unto all. Come out of captivity, break the chain of mental slavery, and false reality, by the grace of GOD. For, who is he that can redeem or awake himself from a false awareness? If you are, thank GOD, fight on for life.

165-Meditation

"BUT WITH RIGHTEOUSNESS SHALL HE JUDGE THE POOR, AND REPROVE WITH EQUITY FOR THE MEEK OF THE EARTH: AND HE SHALL SMITE THE EARTH: WITH THE ROD OF HIS MOUTH, AND WITH THE BREATH OF HIS LIPS SHALL HE SLAY THE WICKED". ISA. 11:4.

166-Meditation

"And shall make him of quick understanding in the fear of the Lord: and he shall not judge after the sight of his eyes, neither reprove after the hearing of his ears:" Isaiah 11:3.

167-Meditation

"And the spirit of the Lord shall rest upon him, the spirit of wisdom and understanding, the spirit of counsel and might, the spirit of knowledge and of the fear of the Lord;" Isa 11:2.

168-Meditation

Humans can love and care for one another whilst desiring the same. When we learn the laws of life we can make the earth the heaven we so desire: an ideal world of freedom, life, love, and happiness for all.

169-Meditation

War is a terrible thing yet when under threat of extinction, conflict becomes inevitable and victory the only choice. Adversaries Of Life are enemies of humanity.

"AND THERE WAS WAR IN HEAVEN: MICHAEL AND HIS ANGELS FOUGHT AGAINST THE DRAGON; AND THE DRAGON FOUGHT AND HIS ANGELS, AND PREVAILED NOT; NEITHER WAS THEIR PLACE FOUND ANY MORE IN HEAVEN. AND THE GREAT DRAGON WAS CAST OUT, THAT OLD SERPENT, CALLED THE DEVIL, AND SATAN, WHICH DECEIVETH THE WHOLE WORLD: HE WAS CAST OUT INTO THE EARTH, AND HIS ANGELS WERE CAST OUT WITH HIM". REV 12:7-9

170-Meditation

Resist evil/devil and it/he will flee. Evil doesn't stop by neglecting or ignoring its existence. The good overcomes it by counteroffensive efforts. You have the law on your side, act now and fast before soon, they become the majority in your own house and overthrow you. Cast out the Devil.

171-Meditation

Without offensive efforts, heaven would not have rid itself of devils and evil. Fight the good fight of faith and for life.

172-Meditation

We are at peace because you have shown restraint, patience, and long-suffering patriots and saints, despite your blood boiling magma and heart racing in disgust at the way the devils are treating your beloved land. Thank you for trusting the Lord and his plan.

173-Meditation

Faith is not believing in the absence of logic and reasoning; without which a believer is prone to deception and believing in something different from what one intends to believe. GOD provides a reason for your faith in life and love for Him through Christ and Nature.

174-Meditation

Fires are not all wild, coincidental and organic nor are they all caused by climate change. Devils too at work.

175-Meditation

To be worthy because you are Rich is vanity and transient. The worthy is rich because he is wealthy. Be rich because you are wealthy but not because of cash in hand. For your riches are the expression of your wealth.

176-Meditation

The standard of living of the people heavily depends on the past and fully or in part on the current leadership and institutions. In part because the current leadership can always improve the lives of the people.

177-Meditation

Irrespective of before or after this life, victim, or victor, born poor or rich, we see so much ignorance, imperfections, evil, and darkness causing hell here in heaven of earth. Grateful for this light found when and how we know not. We will fight on, kindle, and brighten to the end.

178-Meditation

The truth is extreme where a lie reigns supreme, and ignorance is the queen. Blinded, truth becomes hidden in plain sight, seems absent, and is unacceptable.

179-Meditation

What if the poor man's reality is a rich's trick? Interesting to know.
Replace poor with ___
Replace rich with___
Of course, you know _

180-Meditation

It's evil to launch a smear campaign right before or on the day of a man's greatest achievement to defame, deprive, and drown his praise and fuel his hatred among the people. This is just the way of a devil.

181-Meditation

Devils should never be allowed to rule or live in the midst of the Saints. They will change your laws (laws after GOD for a god) and replace good with evil. In the world, good and evil is a matter of law. By law, evil can be called good when devils are the power and influence. Saints, we can't let this happen.

182-Meditation

Now you know why heaven has no place for a devil. Every evil system, society, world, and evil people have expiration dates and time. But the land and life of Saints is eternal. Evil is self-destructive. Death from within by divine design.

183-Meditation

Man's guiding laws at present are not as of the beginning, established in righteousness, equality, peace, and justice. Yet it is good, but not the best. There is a need for a change for the better not for evil.

184-Meditation

There shall be no hiding place for devils in the reign of the righteous. For he rests not until the wicked is exposed and brought to Justice. Exposing may follow Justice when the crime is too shocking to the ordinary. Either way, the Saints will rejoice and trust God's plan.

185-Meditation

Yes, you have GOD-given rights, but they would be trampled upon by your neighbor or he that usurp power over you and do not respect or acknowledge GOD in the first place. You must and others must fight to keep those rights for you and generations to come.

186-Meditation

Don't take him for a fool when he tries to avoid answering valid questions or present his viewpoint but overly shouts, interrupts you from making a point, talk over you, and repeats baseless and made-up accusations and rhetorical sentences.

187-Meditation

"FOR I KNOW THE THOUGHTS AND PLANS THAT I HAVE FOR YOU, SAYS THE LORD, THOUGHTS, AND PLANS FOR WELFARE AND PEACE AND NOT FOR EVIL, TO GIVE YOU HOPE IN YOUR FINAL OUTCOME." JER 29:11

188-Meditation

The mind is so complex such that a word, experience, sound or input from sensory stimuli etch or leave indelible impressions on our soul so much so that they become living and active strongholds controlling, transforming, and influencing the one's thoughts, character or behavior.

189-Meditation

Our consciousness of the greater self has been eroded to think so highly of those leading us as gods, unaccountable with unalienable right and power to rule over us. How did we get here, where those trusted become the adversary?

190-Meditation

Saint is upholding and beholding to the highest ethics, morals, honorary, standards, excellency, integrity towards life and or GOD. Human interaction and society are built on naive belief that the entrusted is forever trustworthy and truthful without continual checks and balances.

200-Meditation

"WASH YOU, MAKE YOU CLEAN; PUT AWAY THE EVIL OF YOUR DOINGS FROM BEFORE MINE EYES; CEASE TO DO EVIL; LEARN TO DO WELL; SEEK JUDGMENT, RELIEVE THE OPPRESSED, JUDGE THE FATHERLESS, PLEAD FOR THE WIDOW." ISAIAH 1:16,17.

201-Meditation

All sins are mistakes but not all mistakes are Sin. Not all sins are unto death just as not all mistakes are fatal. Sin and mistakes are avoidable. Vectors: Horizontal and vertical. Carnal or spiritual both must be avoided by efforts in both realms. Knowledge of GOD and Self.

202-Meditation

No, we don't take the word Saint lightly, and in no way do we cheapen its sacredness by our imperfections. The Saints of the Council are sanctified and continuously evolve into the perfect beings that GOD has made. There are heights and levels to desire and advance.

203-Meditation

How about the rapture was reversed such the devils and the wicked are cleansed/taken from the surface of the earth by the Lord and the Saints? Our greatest task would be turning the hearts of man toward GOD, life. That is the ultimate victory of GOD to end evil. We understand there are dimensions to evil. For without GOD, the arm of justice could be called evil without the context of the crime. Ultimately when the power and capability to do evil, The Law of Sin and Death is destroyed, the life of the Spirit of Christ; love, faith, and righteousness, shall flow within us without any impedance.

204-Meditation

Let's fix leadership and institutions in all nations: the true cause of mass willful or forced immigration.

205-Meditation

We were all tainted by corruption and lies to some extent. Are you awake yet? Are you saved? Help us oh Lord and Saints, our hope.

206-Meditation

Are we born ignorant so that we must learn everything we know here? If we are born ignorant and ignorant of the truth, of life and the universe is sin, is ignorance then an original sin? Think about life and body intelligence or operating system.

207-Meditation

There is darkness or death or ignorance when life's intelligence is turned off. Truth is light and life.

208-Meditation

We are told or learn what we know (some by revelation knowledge). The best decision or solution is by careful analysis of available information from multiple and opposing sources or alternatives not just agreeing sources or information.

209-Meditation

GOD knows good and evil, yet GOD is good and never corrupted or adulterated by Evil. You are not good because you know not the works, devices, or ways of the devil.

210-Meditation

We believe it's a strong mind that can hold and entertain two opposing views without being influenced into animosity and bias towards one. We only choose sides in applying the laws of life. Perception is not the same as conviction.

211-Meditation

We The People Are One from One GOD. WTPA1F1G

212-Meditation

People's finances, health, mind health, and lives are under attack. This is not a joke. Humanity is at war. GOD understands exactly what you are going through. Keep the faith, pray, and never give up on the LORD our GOD. We The People Are One from One GOD.

213-Meditation

In the debate between GOOD and Evil, each side argued their side to be the good according to the prevailing laws of conscience. Thankfully for those we call GOOD the law of the *land is on their side. The GOOD argued they are good by the laws of life, and GOD but the EVIL argued by the laws of gods and man, for they refuse to acknowledge GOD. Thankfully, the prevailing laws of man (land) are good. No wonder the Evil wants to change the laws of the land. Their greatest task has been reshaping the consciousness of mankind. Yes, they succeeded in the past at different places where good today was called evil, and evil was called good. Saints of this age have a duty to continue to keep victories won by other Saints to keep the laws good. We know Jesus Christ will end this war once and for all. Love life. So, Mankind and the other kinds can come to live together under the one law of life; Respect, love, and support for each other.*

214-Meditation

All lives matter. Stand for life. Life (God) has no color. We are all GOD's children. Devils recognizing only their own, refuse to love all lives, seek to divide on every front and faults. Listen to the voice of love and peace. We have a chance to make things right. Know your enemy. Fight for life. A house divided will fall.

215-Meditation

In our age when slavery is abominable, a hindsight of slavery only brings disgust, intolerable, and angry emotions for what blacks have been subjected to all over the world. As a Saint slavery is abominable to GOD no matter the times.

Either in Old Testament or New Testament, GOD hates oppression, violence, manipulation, exploitation of and against all lives. Remember GOD is LOVE.

The Council of the Living Saints know of a history in forgotten memories and in recorded libraries when and where Blacks ruled and had slaves. That's true. Regardless, slavery is evil no matter the time.

216-Meditation

The two-party political system can be an illusion and a great deception to give the people a false hope of choice. This is the case because of the polarity in the minds of man. When the two become one, they select which one to usurp power, alternating parties as necessary to keep the lie. It becomes nearly impossible for a third-party to participate.

217-Meditation

We believe in our country despite her imperfections (devils cloned her and did bad things in her name) because when our country is free, she frees the rest of the world. In silence with her true children, she watched. No more. It appears there are two countries in our country for which one but not her, must die to save our country.

218-Meditation

Do we love any country over the other? No. We love life, people everywhere. What is a country without people? It is the duty of the people to Life (GOD) to make their country a living place because GOD provided in every country enough resources for its people.

219-Meditation

Every nation is a hope of the world we cannot afford to lose. Every nation is a dream we cannot afford to lose. Every nation is a life we cannot afford to lose. Every nation is beautiful. We are the true of the land, we the people. Infiltration instead of invasion. Devils among us. GOD wins.

220-Meditation

Jesus Christ is the savior of the world, our Lord and God

221-Meditation

Change can only be meaningful by legislative or executive law. A society may protect or revolt all it wants but only get things worse if in the end no change is made to leadership to effect the change sought after or change existing laws to facilitate the change requested.

We can only wonder why people who have been in power for so long will only promote protest and riots against no change. Why can't you see your enemy of change?

222-Meditation

People are awake eventually when they rather beg among them the noblest to lead sacrificially instead of the present order of selfish individuals begging to profitably lead people.

223-Meditation

A Saint once said, "I was told that GOD is everywhere but not in me because I AM sinner. That was very conflicting until I began to tell myself in faith that I AM son of GOD. Free now, I

AM righteous, just and love". The consciousness of I AM in Christ is dominion over sin.

224-Meditation

We the people are grateful oh Lord and the Saints forever and ever for your selfless service to the universe. Thank you.

225-Meditation

According to the psychology of Genesis 30:40, there should be a ban on the use of black shooting targets/silhouettes not just for police training.

226-Meditation

Oh, Saints and Lord, the LORD thy GOD is with you fear not and fight, fight, fight. Evil in motion can only be stopped by equal or greater force of Good. The fire of Evil given the world environment extinguishes not on its own. Save life.

227-Meditation

Yes, we all must be Righteously outraged and demand justice and law enforcement reformation but how do we protect the people from the devils who continually start crises for the news cycle and use it, especially at a particular season to their advantage?

The Council Of Living Saints
The Meditations Of A Christian Saint

228-Meditation

Yes, we need a change of authorities, political and judicial systems, and structures. Our law enforcement and positions of power and authority should have zero tolerance for devils.

229-Meditation

Heaven becomes a false hope of a promise to him that fails his duty to life on earth. The false hope of ideal conditions or a perfect world to him that seeks heaven as an escape from the present reality without effort to the present moment what he wishes for.

230-Meditation

Many people realizing the power of lack upon them, the level of evil in the earth or their inability to self-actualize, surrender, and comfort themselves in the belief of a heaven to come. This is not a coincidence. We are not here to do nothing for another world.

231-Meditation

The world is what we make it. Evidently, it has been made by the devil; lack, suffering, hunger, divisions, wars, hate, disasters, crisis …. It is your duty to life to make the world a better place. If not for you at least for the next generation. Yes, I know you believe Jesus is coming soon we also believe, but generation after generation people believed and are no more.

232-Meditation

One must not derelict his duty to life while awaiting the second coming of Jesus.

233-Meditation

Yes, all lives must live but when a devil is allowed to continue in his ways but for a moment, he considers in his ignorance and pride, that there is no GOD to judge and takes our leniency for weakness. Although hardly a devil repents the Lord unfailing in love offers every opportunity for deliverance.

234-Meditation

Yes, all lives must live but a life that takes (steals, kills, and destroys) another selfishly or to advance an evil cause of another group is condemned by the Law of Life. Hard to believe but devils never give up their evil ways for good even when caught or judged.

235-Meditation

At the judgment throne, mercy is there on asking for everyone, just a call away. GOD is GOOD. But sadly, devils blinded by evil, and pride forsake her.

236-Meditation

INVEST, UNLOCK, and CONTROL power in your NAME, TONGUE, DEEDS, and PRESENCE to be a MASTER.

Your NAME: build and guard your honorable reputation. Gain divine power in your name by righteousness, love, and justice. Wherever your name is thought of in the mind or mentioned in the mouth, respect and authority are evoked.

Your WORDS: lack no words to communicate or conceal your thoughts, emotions, and wisdom. Let your WORDS be living. Be a person of your words.

Your DEEDS: let your work be good and excellent, a trademark to testify of you. Price not everything you offer for not every you receive costs you.

Your PRESENCE: Take care of yourself. Let your presence radiate love, peace, and hope. Obey the first law of life. Whatever you do you must survive but it's against the law to expend another's life for your survival. It's great love to give or risk your life for others' survival.

237-Meditation

There appears to be a nation of the Elite (the ruling class) and a nation of people in every country struggling to survive.

238-Meditation

Think about it. Was the COVID prediction a warning, bait, blackmail, threat, or genuine concern?

Does God know the past present and future events?

239-Meditation

Saints Are All Patriots.

240-Meditation

When it comes to inflection warfare it is not just an attack on your health but your rights and liberties, life and livelihood, conscience, and the very soul of humanity. Who is our savior but our Lord and his Saints, our very present help?

241-Meditation

Guard your child from conception against demonic possession and teach him/her to continue when of age. Cease not to pray for your children or your people. A prayer for others always pays back multiple folds.

242-Meditation

The will to live, the quest for an equal chance to life, the clave for love, the thirst for justice, and the dream of freedom are human, above any seemingly divide, race, ethnicity, or religion that we associate or find ourselves. A Saint is a God-sent savior. We are all from somewhere/something/someone we must be saved.

243-Meditation

What's prayer?
By your faith or level of maturity in Christ:
1. Communication with God.
2. Participation in spiritual warfare
3. Summoning, consultation of spirits
4. Petitioning God
5. Focusing, converging of spirit, mind, and body to create a cause.
6. Act of worship: rituals and ceremonial reverence.
7. Process of affecting or adding thought to universal consciousnesses. It's all about your posture and disposition at Prayer. We all pray one way or the other. But to whom and how?

Prayer is the harnessing from GOD or bringing from within power to effect a change or a cause. " ...THE HEARTFELT AND PERSISTENT PRAYER OF A RIGHTEOUS MAN CAN ACCOMPLISH MUCH [WHEN PUT INTO ACTION AND MADE EFFECTIVE BY GOD—IT IS DYNAMIC AND CAN HAVE TREMENDOUS POWER]. Jam 5:16.

244-Meditation

To every Saint this is a purpose of living: to fight the good fight of faith and overcome evil within and without. And when won never let your guard down as before in time past, evil will cease not to exist among the living.

245-Meditation

The earnest expectation of all Saints, especially those not physically engaged in the battlefield or at the forefront, is to see the end of devils and the reign of peace, life, joy, prosperity, and ascension to the greater self. Read Romans 8:19.

246-Meditation

The slogan for every angel; For GOD and heaven. And so, this is for every man. We battle no other country but the common evil in our countries and against our country.

247-Meditation

There can be forgiveness in, after, or through chastisement, correction, penitentiary, and mercy depending on who, what, and the extent of the offense. Remember those that the Lord loves he chastises (Read Heb 12:6). Guess what he will do to His enemies. You can be forgiven and still pay the price of penance.

A price not to destroy you, not harm you, and not always a pain but a price consequential or by design to save you from a destructive end (eternal condemnation), to eventually develop, refine, and mature you.

248-Meditation

Experience they say is the best teacher, but true, only to the one with a teachable and wise spirit. Many a time many people go through life's university or a repetitive experience without learning a thing. It's repetitive because maybe you are not learning from it. Suffer to give the children the best experiences in the now.

249-Meditation

Forgiveness is conditional without forgetfulness and repetition. Our GOD is a God of love but of vengeance and justice. He who stops a friend or a foe from repeating a wrong against him saves himself and the assailant. Resist evil and also, resist the devil. To forgive and love unconditionally is divine.

250-Meditation

How sad it is that people are made to look up to a world of peace, prosperity, and freedom to come without contributing to its making at least for future generations. This mindset is by design.

251-Meditation

The world, like many worlds before this but the same earth, is destroyed by evil. A new world is upon us as always created and only sustained by good.

252-Meditation

Think about it I fear not my enemy that is with me, without power and influence but that enemy who is far off but has power and influence. Do you see what this means? You see why in this world the first victory of Satan was to dethrone man and dominate or put his people in power.

253-Meditation

Asked what if the Gods are aliens? Define Alien, then yes, but not by definition, far from how you understand the word.

254-Meditation

Satan can never rule humanity without devils. Jesus will never win without the Saints. Never let a devil rule over you. Sin (devils) shall not have dominion over you. Resist!

255-Meditation

He who takes away man's right to defend himself consequentially gives the right of destruction to his enemy. He is not just an enabler but a culprit. Who is vulnerable and defenseless? Who is he that prey on the defenseless? Oh, Saint fight the good fight of faith, it is your duty to life.

256-Meditation

Words represent MEANING. No word in itself can adequately represent or express an assigned meaning or significance. LIMITATIONS of language to Spirit. You know more than you can express in words. Know that a heard word was first a thought, then a sound before a language.

If we think (formulate ideas, reason) in words it's important that we are not limited in words (vocabularies).

257-Meditation

Yes, in the family of the grass plant man can have a sustainable source of food and medicine.

258-Meditation

I looked and the high places of the devils were no more. Pray oh prey that you prey no more to devils.

259-Meditation

We are individuals of all ages and walks of life who believe in life on earth and life to come. A Saint has greater love, for greater love has no man than to lay his life for that of another. A devil may die for another of his own kind but unlike Christ and a Saint, all lives are equal and worth dying for. For them, it's survival of the fittest, elitists, superiors, and royals. That's exactly how evil is defined for we all are of GOD and should strive to develop and sustain each other. We are Saints.

260-Meditation

This is our land our planet and our world. This we will protect against all enemies both physical and spiritual. This we will defend against all forces, both spirits or creatures, against all, both visible and invincible. GOD help us.

261-Meditation

Prayers for all victims of COVID-19-related attacks in body and soul for our war is not just physical. Be healed now in JESUS Christ's name.

262-Meditation

Price not everything you give for not all you receive costs you.

263-Meditation

We pray for our military and law enforcers. You are at the forefront of the battle here and to come. You are defending, and protecting the dignity and sanctity of humanity by implementing justice of the righteousness judgment.

264-Meditation

It is not in your power to show mercy to him who no mercy was given at the righteousness judgment or show weakness of favoritism or partiality, then you will be guilty as culprits of the wicked and evil ones. Take heart for your strength is of GOD who called you in his time.

265-Meditation

In our prayers today we shared our life (energy, force, spirit) with the Saints at the war front in this battle to save humanity. Like the apostles would say "With you in spirit", we may not know what you are doing now or understand it, yet we trust our Lord and the saving plan.

266-Meditation

Tonight, we continue to lift our voices and hearts in prayers to GOD our life in all reverence, praise, and thanksgiving for although the devils meant it for our destruction GOD has turned it for our GOOD and the end of them. The Lord our God is GOOD.

267-Meditation

I cannot express my gratitude enough for the leadership that called for National prayers in end times and a crucial time like this. Imagine the quality and quantity of prayer incense that was received in heaven today. Awesome. Hasn't happened in centuries. Thank you all.

268-Meditation

On this day of National oh GOD may our prayer offerings be acceptable in your sight and heal our land and the world. Thank you for the lives of our Lord and the saving work of the Saints in times like this.

269-Meditation

To cease to pray is to cease to prosper.

The Council Of Living Saints
The Meditations Of A Christian Saint

270-Meditation

Humanity has been fighting the Serpent, dragon, beast, and demon race of devils literally from the beginning. "And I will put enmity between thee and the woman, and between thy seed and her seed; it shall bruise thy head, and thou shalt bruise his heel."

271-Meditation

We know that by the law of life, GOD is GOOD and GOOD is life. So evil is death to life and good is all life unto life.

272-Meditation

GOD created you but man made you. We know the GOD that created you but who's the MAN or creature that made you?

273-Meditation

Moses was given 10 commandments, Jesus gave us ten-in-two, but we are given one-in-two. You must live without taking another's life for your life. All lives must live without expending other's lives. This is love, to give or risk your life that others may live. By this the righteous and wise judge.

Life is:

Your very living essence in matter

Your unalienable rights

Your living possessions

Everything that adds to living essence, life force, spirit, growth ...

274-Meditation

You are not a Saint because you are ignorant of the schemes and plans of devils. You are righteous and holy because you exercise restraint and choose to do GOOD in the face of temptation or coercion. For GOD knows evils but cannot be overcome by evil.

275-Meditation

For every ACTION there is a REACTION so for every CAUSE there is an EFFECT. An effect may stem from multiple causes so can a cause evoke ripple effects. A room full of smelling trash is masked with air freshener. Cause: trash, Effect: smell. Sadly, you worry only about the effect whilst the trash remains.

276-Meditation

When it comes to misinformation, disinformation, information control, and psychological warfare to deceive and control a people, it's a matter of battle for the soul and the fate of it hereafter.

277-Meditation

The Devil hate order, harmony, and joy of a free prosperous society (people) such that he covertly creates crisis, disasters, problems, and chaos and then control the effect and narrative while promising solutions feigning sympathy and affection for his victims and society. A devil's modus operandi.

The Council Of Living Saints
The Meditations Of A Christian Saint

278-Meditation

We carry along with us our experiences and knowledge acquired engrained in our self (DNA) to be passed on. Never be ignorant and strive for the best and most noble experiences at least to affect positively your generations to come.

279-Meditation

Your victory over evil in the battle of GOOD and Evil is from your ability to know and anticipate every move of the enemy and the wisdom to timely countermove. GOD is GOOD and omniscient! With GOD victory belongs to our God.

280-Meditation

It's inconsistent with life to be against abortion but unconcerned or an enabler of human trafficking, slavery, and abuse. Don't be a hypocrite for the fight for life doesn't end with first breadths but until and after your last.

281-Meditation

Praying for people all over the world especially places of concern right now. May GOD help the responders, families affected and the warriors of GOOD fighting evil in these countries.

282-Meditation

We thank GOD and are forever grateful to our Lord for the safety of all our people all over the world. We still pray and thank the Lord in whom we trust for peace.

283-Meditation

The truly educated is one who has applied knowledge and understanding of the worlds, and their workings. There are levels of mind and sight.

284-Meditation

Life is full of challenges, not all in the negative sense. Don't give up on your fight for life. Your reward is not of man. It's not a coincidence that you are in this alive. You are more than a conqueror. GOD is with/in you. You are not alone.

285-Meditation

Thank you, all Saints, for fighting for the people. Forgive them, they don't know and understand what and who you are up against. For if they did they would worship you as Gods.

286-Meditation

In creation, the birth of evil creates simultaneously timed self-destructive mechanisms activated by good and a righteous judge, for the harmony and possible salvation of the host and universe. GOD's love for His creation.

287-Meditation

What is the Bible?
A Bible (by definition) is the collection of scriptures or spiritual books.
What is Scripture?

Scripture is a writing inspired by the Spirit (Divine) or WORD of GOD. Traditionally, these writings were recorded on papyrus sheets.

What is the word of GOD?
GOD's communication to creatures. In the context of the Bible, it is the statement or word related to Christ. We have written and non-written, spoken, and unspoken word of GOD. To include nature, creatures, dreams, visions...
From the Word of GOD, we get Scriptures and out of Scriptures we get the Bible.
A person who places his or her faith in the Bible inherently must have trusted the sincerity, reliability, and obedience to GOD of those who compiled and translated it.

288-Meditation

People are indeed guided by two fundamental forces: love and law. Without a genuine sense of love, compassion, or respect for one another, and regard for just and ethical laws, an individual can become a disruptive force within society and potentially pose a danger to the broader universe.

It's worth noting that love, in its various forms, can foster cooperation, empathy, and unity among people. Meanwhile, law, when based on principles that uphold justice, equality, and the sanctity of life, can establish a framework for peaceful coexistence and the protection of individual rights.

Aligning laws with the principles of love, compassion, and the preservation of life is a noble aspiration. Ensuring that every individual can live without causing harm to others is a fundamental goal of many ethical and legal systems. Such principles can contribute to a more just and harmonious society, reflecting values that prioritize the well-being, dignity, and rights of every individual without infringing on the lives of others. This approach aligns with principles of justice, fairness, and the promotion of harmonious coexistence within society and, by extension, the broader universe.

289-Meditation

The desire for self-actualization, achieving true success and freedom, yields profound satisfaction, akin to the intensity of sexual desire. Substituting the former with the latter is a travesty, and the deliberate attempt to suppress one's aspiration for GOOD success or manipulate another to prioritize sexual desire over it is considered unethical and evil. A child growing toward a life of GOOD success reflects the divine grace of GOD. We extend my heartfelt gratitude to the Lord and to all the courageous individuals, Saints, whether civilian or military, who risk their lives in the pursuit of GOOD success for all. Stay resolute, and have faith in GOD's plan to save nations.

290-Meditation

A soul tainted by corruption is abhorrent to GOD and disruptive to the harmony and consciousness of the universe.

291-Meditation

Oh, Saint, it's in your very nature to use the instrument of love, mercy, righteousness, and justice in your fight against evil without hate. Failure to overcome the evil within is not an option, or else you will be called the devil.

The Council Of Living Saints
The Meditations Of A Christian Saint

292-Meditation

You are not GOOD because you are suffering long-suffering, helpless, and defenseless in the face of abuse, injustice, and ill-treatment. You are good because you fight back, resist, and stop evil. It's wisdom to endure but for a while if it's strategic to expose, resist, and defeat evil.

293-Meditation

We are thankful for life (GOD), for family, for country, and for the people of life.

294-Meditation

To many, prayer is perceived as a form of labor and an active effort by a worshipper or a creature. However, there exist prayers of inaction, where your needs, struggles, trials, circumstances, and life itself beseech or communicate with GOD for His intervention or prompting a response independent of your direct supplication.

Indeed, GOD's love is unconditional, just as life and consciousness are bestowed upon us without our request. Keep in mind that GOD cares for and provides for all His creation, whether one acknowledges, loves, or disapproves of Him—His faithfulness remains unwavering, and endures eternally.

However, the gods are not all like GOD. They are not all loving, merciful, and gracious. They are at war with each other (or so appears to man) and require worshippers to take a side. There is a god at every place of worship that answers according to their faithfulness and the power of the god.

There is but one GOD, the only true God.

295-Meditation

Success indeed holds varying meanings for different individuals, yet it often embodies the "attainment of a valuable aspiration." It materializes from a notion, concept, or objective. It reflects your capacity to surmount obstacles, secure the necessary resources, and employ the required methods to reach such a target or conclusion.

Success can indeed be evaluated through moral or societal standards and the perspective of GOD. May you achieve a GOOD and a BAD success. GOOD success enhances or advances both the individual and humanity, offering freedom in time and finances, as well as fostering peace, love, and joy. Good success is life unto life, breathing life into life itself.

296-Meditation

Desires should not always be seen in a negative light. Desires drive us to alter our current state or circumstances. Without desire, there would be no motivation for progress or growth. Our desires can be swayed, misguided, or molded by external influences, including other people and our surroundings. It is crucial to be mindful of our desires and aim for those that promote and enrich life, both for ourselves and those around us. Keep in mind that three fundamental and vital elements for internal change are desires, willpower, and faith.

The Council Of Living Saints
The Meditations Of A Christian Saint

297-Meditation

One of the greatest acts of goodness an individual can do for themselves, for their past, present, and future, as well as for humanity as a whole, is to actively support a GOOD leader and firmly resist a BAD one. It is essential to recognize that not all in leadership positions are humans, who exhibit human values. It's no surprise that a nation, that values the principles of justice and humanity, may resist leaders who do not uphold these values.

Leaders rule by systems they or their predecessors make. The standard of living of the people depends on these. In the age of ignorance or great deception and indifference of the people, these powerful systems in the hands of a BAD leader are destructive to humanity and the world.

we hold this to be true that not all Leaders are the choice of the people yet are made conscientiously and uncontentiously to follow. Their ignorance and indifference to governance have paved the way to the Biblical apocalypse. Who can save but GOD, not a man God but GOD man.

298-Meditation

"WHEN JUSTICE IS DONE, IT IS A JOY TO THE RIGHTEOUS (THE UPRIGHT, THE ONE IN RIGHT STANDING WITH GOD), BUT TO THE EVILDOERS IT IS DISASTER."
PROV 21:15

299-Meditation

The Evil knows no limit except the one imposed by the Good. Stop the Evil, Good! You are known for stopping evil. Then your true self would be known when evil is no more.

300-Meditation

The battle against Satan is for GOD. The battle against demons is for Angels/Watchers so is the battle against devils is for Christ/Saints. These battles are not for Christians. Is there a difference between a Christian and a Saint? Which are you?

Wow unto you if you are a mere human (the indifferent) or just the follower on these battlefields. For the canal man is but nothing or an instrument of war (victims of the battlefield) in the battlefield of the gods.

Made in the USA
Columbia, SC
09 October 2024